Lord, RIDE with me today

The story of a solo coast-to-coast bicycle journey

DAVID FREEZE

Published by:
Walnut Creek Farm Publishing
China Grove, NC 28023

Designed by Andy Mooney
Map illustration by Andy Mooney
Cover photography by Jon C. Lakey

ISBN 978-0-578-13376-8

FOREWORD

David Freeze and I first crossed paths when my church youth group was organizing a 5K race to raise funds for a mission trip. We needed an expert and, as head of the local runners club for over a decade, David is the local authority on all things running.

He runs marathons. He organizes races. He trains beginning runners.

David is so associated with running that many of his acquaintances were surprised when he announced in the spring of 2013 that he would embark on a cross-country bicycle trip in the summer, pedaling more than 4,000 miles from coast to coast. But we should have seen it coming. In 2009, he had shared a column with the Salisbury Post, chronicling a three-day bicycle trip on the Greenbriar Trail in West Virginia. It was beautifully written; David is a born storyteller. But the experience gave him more than another tale to tell; it planted a seed.

He ended that column with words of advice for anyone having second thoughts about tackling a big adventure "There will always be an excuse," he wrote. "Just go!"

So in the summer of 2013, David just went — this time with a iPad in his pack so he could send nightly dispatches to the Salisbury Post.

We were more than happy to have his stories and photos, but it wasn't until David dipped the back wheel of his bike in the Pacific and set off that the real magnitude of what he was tackling became clear to those of us back home. It was a long solo journey through all kinds of terrain and weather.

On the second day of the trip, he wrote about sharing the road in Oregon with huge logging trucks. That sparked mental images of David — 5-foot-9 and 145 pounds — pedaling his bike alongside monster trucks swaying with heavy loads. This ride would be more than an adventure, we realized. It would test David's endurance and courage.

Post readers were right there with David as he climbed steep mountains and crossed windy plains, going through cold rain at one point and, just days later, heat so fierce that sweat dripped off his elbows. He persevered through long, lonely stretches without any place to buy food or water for miles and miles.

The further along David got into his trip, the greater the number of people following his progress through the Post and online. Many who followed his travels sent up prayers and emailed encouraging messages. Even under stress from heat or harrowing experiences, he sent reports that were light-hearted, chatty and rich with local color.

While we read of David's adventures from the comfort of our desks and easy chairs, he was burning 7,000 calories a day, hauling up to 40 pounds of supplies and pedaling 10 hours a day.

We learned a lot about the country, and we learned a lot about David — including what he likes to eat. Pancakes, Pop-Tarts and pizza. Brownies and bananas. Reese's Cups. And ice cream, ice cream, ice cream. Though Freeze was not much of an ice cream eater before the trip, the frozen dessert hit the spot like nothing else on this trip. He even started using the phrase, "my first ice cream of the day."

After David finally put his front tire in the Atlantic Ocean and returned home, the Post sponsored an ice-cream social in his honor that drew more than 200 people. People were hungry for more de-tails, and he was glad to share them. But he wisely decided to do his re-telling all at once in this book, which includes the material from his columns and many more specifics about the challenges and mis-haps he experienced. It's a warts-and-all description of what a cy-clist can expect on a cross-country trek.

Though he says he always expects to see a 30-year-old in the mirror, David was in fact a very fit and athletic 60 when he took this journey. But it's outlook and energy that really tell our age, and David has a lot going for him on those fronts. Through his daily reports from the road and now this book, David shows what it takes to set an audacious goal and make it happen. Preparation. Optimism. Perseverance. If you have all those qualities and you're thinking about tackling a similar trip, you can bet money on what David would advise.

Just go.

— **Elizabeth Cook**
Editor, Salisbury Post

ACKNOWLEDGMENTS

It was a great honor to work with lots of talented people as this book has come to life. Since this is my first book, I needed the input of many knowledgeable people. I found them at every turn. Thanks to Edward Norvell and Kurt Corriher, local authors, for their input as I began to put together a plan. Deal Safrit pushed me in the right direction when I needed it. A huge special thank you to Joe Ellis, an accomplished author and running friend from Martin's Ferry, Ohio, for input all the way from editing to final printing and distribution. I couldn't have put the book together without the work of my friends from the Salisbury Post, Editor Elizabeth Cook for editing and contributions to the book, Andy Mooney for his fantastic design and layout, and the always awesome photography from Jon C. Lakey. Those who took their time to edit my work were Norma Patterson, Cora Shinn, Joan Cress and Susan Shinn, who put it all together. I can't say enough about all the encouragement from those who followed my ride from Rowan County and surrounding areas, and sent prayers and encouragement as I rode across America and then again as we put the book together. A special acknowledgment to Jane Patterson for being a great friend, confidant and sounding board through both the ride and the book. And to my daughters, Ashley and Amber, thanks for being there through it all, and know that I love you both very much.

INTRODUCTION

After months of putting it off, I set out for what I thought would be a great chance to get outdoors in a new way. I wanted a challenge, to see large sections of unspoiled land, and to test myself. This trip seemed perfect: not too long, yet still exciting.

I drove north toward West Virginia on Interstate 77. Rain was falling and it was still dark. My bike was in the back of my truck, and my gear was up front with me. The anticipation, the apprehension and the thoughts of a new adventure fueled my early-morning ride toward the Greenbrier River.

Never had I thought of going into the wilderness, or even this far from home, for a long bike ride. Would I like it as much as I thought? Could I handle the physical challenge of riding for up to 60 miles a day? Would the elements take a toll? Was I crazy to do this?

After finding the trail head, I unloaded the bike and strapped on my gear. This would be my first time to ride a loaded bike. I wondered how much the extra weight would matter and if I could pedal at a good speed with that weight on board. Would I be able to follow the trail and handle any issues that might come up, especially mechanical ones?

I loaded up the bike and secured my truck. It was time to go. I looked back to double-check my gear, and raised my leg to mount the bike — then fell completely over the other side, my bike on top of me.

Was I out of place here? I had not practiced mounting a loaded bike and quickly realized my mistake. Back on my feet and ready to roll, I positioned my feet better and properly mounted the bike and pulled away. The trip was on. No backing out now.

During the three-day ride, I experienced rain, cold and snow, and fatigue caused my neck and shoulders to scream for relief. I ate huge amounts of food as I rode through the wilderness, expending 7,000 calories a day. I slept the sleep of the worn-out dead. Rising in the morning was yet another challenge, tough enough for three days in a row. And that bike seat ...

But the rewards! I saw rustic areas at their purest, and realized that the physical challenge was doable. Sitting on a bike, with eyes wide open, enjoying back-road America! I wanted more, lots more.

An idea was born.

Astoria, Ore.

— 4,164 total miles —

Myrtle
Beach,
S.C.

Chapter 1
— Preparation —

Did I have everything I needed?

You would think that I could set the alarm clock right on the eve of one of the biggest adventures of my life. On Saturday night, June 8, 2013, I had packed the final things for my carry-on for a flight to Portland, Oregon. All of my big gear had already been shipped to Astoria, Oregon, to my destination of the Lamplighter Motel. My winter clothes, my panniers (bike saddle bags), tools, energy bars and riding attire were all there, waiting for me to arrive. My Surly Long Haul Trucker bike was at Bikes and Beyond, also in Astoria. The Surly would be my transportation for nearly 4,200 miles on my journey across America.

Two years of planning culminated in shipping my gear out to the West Coast. Following the great bike trip to West Virginia and the Greenbrier River Trail, I got a small idea that gained unstoppable momentum. If three days on a secluded river could be that much fun, would a bicycle trip across America not be the trip of a lifetime? I saw nature's beauty in rain, snow and beautiful weather. That short ride had included warnings of bear and other wildlife, as well as plenty of brushes with history. I wanted more of the same.

That Saturday night in June, I lay down with little worry about having forgotten something. I knew my fitness level was high, having been running around 200 miles per month and biking about the same. Running has been my passion since 1979, and I've logged just over 70,000 road miles. I was a highly competitive runner for about 30 years, having completed 24 marathons and close to 1,000 other races. Arthroscopic knee surgery in February 2012 had delayed the start of my great adventure, originally scheduled for summer 2012, by a year. Now the time seemed right.

One of my current vocations is a running coach, and I'm often accused of specializing in motivation. The thought of this trip was motivating me already, and I couldn't wait to get started. Another vocation is as a freelance writer for the Salisbury Post in Salisbury, N.C., our local newspaper. My major goal from the start was to journal the whole trip, holding all those spectacular sights and happenings in more than just my memory.

Part of my preparations had included a long talk with the son of a running client who had already crossed the TransAmerica Trail and who had also done the Great Divide bike trail from Mexico to Canada. Andrew Sufficool proved a wealth of knowledge, providing a practical and economical view of what tools, gear and clothing that I should need. Andrew had traveled east to west across America with his brother Matt in 2011. He decided that they carried too much weight on the first trip, and gave me pointers on what to take as must-haves and other possible items if I was willing to pedal the extra weight up the Pacific hills, and eventually the Cascades, the Rockies, the Ozarks and the Appalachians.

Andrew advised me on the choice of a Surly Long Haul Trucker. He uses one, and kept abreast of other models on the market. Following the West Virginia trip, I knew that I would need to upgrade my bike to one that could take the abuse of a long ride and also carry the weight of the survival essentials that would be strapped on the bike. I decided to buy my Surly at Skinny Wheels Bike Shop in Mocksville, N.C. The bike order was one of the final pieces that sealed the deal and locked in the upcoming trip. The bike arrived, and as any good bike shop owner should do, Eric Phillips took about an hour and a half making sure that the seat, handlebars, and the extension of the bike fit my frame. I completed about 300 training miles to make sure it was fitted correctly, and Eric made a few final adjustments before shipping the bike to Astoria.

One thing I really paid attention to on the bike was its seat. In all my riding over the years, I had never found a comfortable seat. Lots of regular riders suggested a Brooks saddle, so I started checking on the reviews for the top-flight leather saddle. Most reviews were positive, but nearly all said that it would take at least 500 miles to break in the seat. To riders who haven't had a Brooks saddle, they seem so hard upon arrival. I certainly wondered if any amount of leather treatment would soften it so that 10-12 hours a day would not have me battling saddle sores throughout the trip. I started treating the seat as soon as I got it, and planned to keep it up throughout the length of my cross-country trip.

Other final decisions that confirmed the trip included ordering the plane ticket to Portland. I got a great deal on a one-way flight. My motel reservation in Astoria was set, and I thought my transportation from Portland to Astoria was also in place. Amtrak operates a bus on that route twice a day at an economical rate. My maps from Adventure Cycling were all packed and ready to go. These maps provide information on following the route east from Astoria. Among the information included were all the road turns and distances for each area, as well as available motels, campgrounds, libraries, bike shops, grocery stores and convenience stores. There was also information on what climate to expect, plus tips on road conditions. I made a final call to Bikes and Beyond, reminding them that I would be there before 4 p.m. on Sunday, June 9. At that time, we would make final adjustments and I would be ready to ride first thing Monday morning.

My two daughters were willing to take me to Spartanburg, S.C. We needed to arrive by 5:30 a.m., which meant an early start. I fell asleep that Saturday night with the expectation of having everything in place.

So much for best laid plans

Nothing was easy on Sunday. I overslept and woke up when my daughters came in the house. With just 15 minutes to spare, I rushed around gathering up my important papers and getting out to the car for the trip to Spartanburg. Finally I was comfortable that I had

3

everything, and settled in for the less than two-hour ride.

I said goodbye with much emotion to the girls outside the airport, realizing that it would probably be 9-10 weeks before I would see them again. We would stay in touch and I planned to copy them on my daily journal, but admittedly we shed a few tears in that early-morning darkness outside the airport.

As harried as my oversleeping caused the ride to be, the day soon took a dramatic change — for the worse. My flight was set to go to Detroit, then on to Portland with a late-morning arrival. We backed away from the gate on time, sat there for about 15 minutes, and then were told that the plane had a safety light that would not go off. A mechanic would have to check it, and, surprisingly, at least to me, there were no mechanics on hand because it was Sunday morning. We were told that the plane may fly later in the day, but the airline would attempt other connections.

I ended up taking four flights that day, finally arriving in Portland at close to 5 p.m., too late for my Amtrak bus connection to Astoria. My options included getting a room until morning, then taking the first bus, and hopefully getting an afternoon start on the ride. The other option was to find another way to Astoria, get there late on Saturday evening, get my bearings and be waiting at the bike shop when it opened on Sunday. I chose to pay a lofty fee for a van ride to cover the hour and a half ride from Portland to Astoria. That ride was scenic and I got close-up views of Mount Hood and Mount St. Helens, Oregon.

I finally arrived in Astoria about 7:30 p.m., certainly too late to get the bike and almost too late to find some food. I did get a huge omelet and hash browns, and settled in to wait for the morning and the opening of Bikes and Beyond. My grand adventure was just hours away.

I awoke with extreme restlessness, so I walked around the beautiful and historic town. The Columbia River empties into the Pacific Ocean near here, and the town is historically significant as the oldest permanent white settlement west of the Mississippi. Astoria's Fort Stevens gained notoriety as being the only military post to be attacked by a foreign enemy since the War of 1812. Fort Stevens was the target of a 17-round cannon attack from a Japanese submarine during World War II.

Bikes and Beyond opened just before 11, and the bike wasn't quite ready to go. Additionally, one of the boxes shipped with it was nowhere to be found. The mechanic made some adjustments and then installed a map holder, a pump and a bike cable lock. I got a couple extra tire tubes and seemed almost ready. After a shakedown ride, I was confident and headed back to the motel to get my stuff. I would be on my way in minutes!

CHAPTER 2
— Astoria to Grande Ronde, Oregon —

Finally on the road

After years of planning, it was time for the real adventure to begin. I made sure to pause for prayer that God would ride with me for every minute of the ride. One of my most touching notes received before I left home hit the nail on the head: "Have a great trip! Have fun, but please be safe and come home in one piece! Talk to the Lord every day and He will ride with you and keep you safe." I looked forward to the ride together.

I snapped on the panniers and bungeed my tent and sleeping bag on the bike. As I checked out of the motel, I was elated. I was going to get to see America, meet many new people, and live an experience that most people only dream about. My dream had come down to this day. I couldn't wait to live this great adventure. I was apprehensive, but my excitement at seeing the bike loaded and ready to roll pushed any disconcerting thoughts to the back burner.

Map 1 from Adventure Cycling was one of the more confusing maps, but I was pretty sure of the right route out of town toward the sacred rear-wheel dipping that would signify the official beginning of my cross-country trip.

It was already after noon, but the temperature was moderate and there was a gentle breeze blowing. I was so excited to get started that I didn't take time yet to analyze where I might spend the night. I had been uncertain about my departure time, but there was riding to do, and that wheel needed to be dipped in the Pacific. I would find a place to spend the night.

The first few turns out of Astoria were surprisingly difficult, especially for a coastal town. I climbed a significant and steep small hill, and my reward was a close-up encounter with a deer standing in the roadway and a fantastic view of the Columbia River as it spilled into the Pacific Ocean. That climb was challenging and I struggled to get to the top. Right away, I wondered if I had what it takes to climb the huge mountains later in the Cascades and Rockies.

Upon leaving Astoria, the TransAmerica Trail heads through Miles Crossing and then across country to Seaside Beach. This is a ride of less than 20 miles, but I soon realized two things. My cyclometer (bicycle odometer) was not working and the roads had wood chips lying everywhere. The cyclometer needed a bike shop, otherwise I couldn't keep up with the miles and the expectations of when to turn left or right, or even on to a new road. I'd have to avoid wood chips from the endless logging trucks that ran the same roads on Monday through Friday. On this Sunday afternoon, the traffic wasn't bad, and the weather remained pleasant.

Originally, I planned to visit Sunset Beach, but eventually headed toward Seaside Beach for the wheel dipping. Seaside Beach was on the mapped route and a resident told me that the beach had easy access. I stopped first at a bike shop to get the cyclometer repaired. All it took was a minor adjustment in the positioning of the meter and that allowed the battery to seal properly. The bike shop didn't charge me for their work or advice, marking the first of many times that I experienced a helpful and giving attitude from those I encountered. My cyclometer was now ready to record the miles and would give me no more trouble throughout the journey. I couldn't wait to go dip my rear wheel, and the beach was just about three blocks from the bike shop. I parked on the edge of the sand, unloaded the panniers, the tent and the sleeping bag, and set about carrying the bike to the edge of the waves.

There are huge differences in Atlantic and Pacific beaches. Pacific beaches are often rocky and nowhere near as flat as their Atlantic counterparts, plus they are potentially cold, even in mid-June. This day was cool and sunny, with almost no breeze. While carrying the bike close to 500 feet to get to the waves, I experienced one of the first comical moments of my trip. The sand seemed well packed, so I left my running shoes on as I began to make the long trek down to the water. I also carried my iPad Mini to take the picture, and thought I could actually hold the bike up and take the picture myself. The bike shop owner had confirmed my thoughts when he advised me not to roll the bike on the sand, but to carry it. No need to let sand or salt mess up the inner workings of the gears. After finally arriving at the water, every time I got set to take the picture, waves would wash over my shoes. I struggled about 10 minutes, getting wetter and wetter, and finally got a lady to take my picture. She kept her distance though, not sure why anyone would want to ride across the country and what that had to do with getting the bike wet in the ocean.

I was traveling light. That one pair of shoes was all I had. It took me a couple of days to get them dry and a couple of weeks to get all the sand out of them.

Once loaded up and rolling again, I began to climb along the Pacific. The Pacific Highlands are a series of 800 to 1,000-foot-high hills that can be steep but offer exciting views of the ocean. Repeatedly, I climbed the hills and immediately coasted back down to sea level on the other side. Later, I realized how much more I liked to climb, then hold an altitude before climbing some more, rather than the roller coaster riding that was planned on the maps.

The objects of the logging industry, the huge Douglas firs that grow in the area, provided thick rain forest canopies along the sides of the road. Logging trucks were now on every road I traveled. Another constant was the huckleberry plant. They grow wild on the roadsides, although they were just blooming when I rode through Oregon in mid-June. Huckleberries are similar to the North Carolina native blackberries. I plan to plant some huckleberries on my farm. They were a part of a nice treat that I grew accustomed to.

Some of the Pacific Hills are used by the locals for whale watching. I was intrigued by the huge rocks that are abundant in the Cannon Beach area. Summer vacationers were wearing sweaters and jackets, and often raincoats as the rain began to be a constant companion. I wore cotton gloves over my leather cycling gloves to help keep my hands warm until the cotton ones became wet, too.

Sunday afternoon's first day ride was only good for about 33 miles, as I left the bike shop much later than I had hoped. Monday's total improved to about 58 miles, and with it I gained some confidence. I had a motel room in Netarts, Oregon, on Monday afternoon with a great view of the rainy Pacific. Early Tuesday, I had my first mishap. Balancing a heavily loaded touring bike is not easy. My legs were just long enough to hike one up and over the panniers, tent and sleeping bag on the back. I stopped just east of Netarts, and decided to get something out of one of the bags. As I lifted my leg to pull it over, the whole bike tumbled down on me as I fell hard on the pavement. While riding, I wore light leather cycling gloves to protect my hands and just a small part of my fingers. The fingertips on each hand are cut out, and those fingertips bore the brunt of this fall. I tried to catch myself, but the pavement peeled back huge amounts of skin. Band-Aids did little to help, but at least provided a protective cover over the damaged fingertips.

On Tuesday, after completing 65 miles, I camped for the first time near Grande Ronde, Oregon, along a stream on the edge of a campground. I didn't pay for the camping because I got to the campground after the office closed, didn't get any of the pass codes for restrooms, showers or Wi-Fi, and was gone way early in the morning before the office opened. I thought later that I should have left some money and a note explaining myself. My meal on Tuesday evening consisted of Pop-Tarts from a convenience store, and grapes and bananas from a produce stand. I soon found that this was not enough for fuel after the long hours on the bike saddle. My first camping experience was not a good one. I didn't sleep well, was hungry all night and fought a leaking tent. Rain set in as a regular companion for much of the next 10 days.

CHAPTER 3
—Grande Ronde to Coburg, Oregon —

Starting to build confidence

Most of the store owners along the way welcomed the cyclists. I didn't expect this. Often, they had specials listed "For Cyclists Only." Traffic never became too heavy along the coast, and at least on one occasion, I thought for sure I was lost because no other vehicles came by for more than 20 minutes. I walked down a steep gravel road and found a guy on a farm, not knowing what kind of reception I might receive. As would become my regular good fortune on this trip, I found a willing and personable local resident to help me with directions. We discussed my ride, and what to expect for the next portion of the trip, just before I headed out with the assurance of being on the right road.

With three days complete, I was gaining more confidence in my ability to complete the trip. The hills wouldn't get any worse for the first 300 miles, and the weather was not yet extreme. My appetite was extreme, however, and as the daily miles climbed, I knew that I would have to take in more calories. I was already heavy on carbs, needing the sustaining energy to keep rolling for 8-9 hours a day. Longer and more challenging days would come later. My favorite food soon became pizza. Pizza had always been a favorite after long runs in my marathon training, largely because of the high complex carbohydrate content and easy availability. I needed both the calories and the carbs here, too, and didn't often have much time to seek out something else. Some of these days had started to feel like marathons already, stretching on for hours of sameness. But I had a daily goal and destination, which kept the pedals turning.

In my planning, I thought there would be time to eat pancakes just about every day, too. They're one of my favorite foods. But I ate them only sporadically, usually when I was really satisfied with my early-morning mileage. This habit continued throughout the ride. I didn't become an expert in cross-country pancakes.

Other cyclists were meeting me heading west, and I spoke to several who were riding the Pacific coast from Canada to California. I found other cyclists friendly, but since we did not have a common destination, there was little logistically for us to discuss.

So far, I had been riding along the Pacific coast every day, but was soon to turn northeast toward the middle of Oregon. I had cycled through lots of small towns near the beaches including Manhattan Beach, Rockaway Beach, Bay City, Tillamook, Ocean Side and Pacific City. Just before Tillamook, I had to pull off the road because traffic was heavy. Once again, I thought that some food would be nice. I had walked the bike to the side of the road, then started to dismount and hooked my foot on the top of the sleeping bag. I fell hard again, and the same fingers were now ripped open again. There was almost no skin left on two of them and blood was dripping off the most injured ones. Traffic had come to a stop when I got up, and one guy came over to see if I was OK. I assured him that I was, and vowed to figure out my dismounting problem.

Tillamook was my favorite of all the towns near the beaches. I hit town on a long and rainy flat stretch, then stopped for a wonderful lunch of an omelet and pancakes. Tillamook is the home of the purportedly largest wooden building in the world, now used as a World War II naval aircraft museum. On the ride through Tillamook, the improved terrain allowed me to complete a total distance of 79 miles for the day, my best yet. There was a steady and cold rain that afternoon, but nothing that slowed my pace.

As a farmer, I was interested in the Willamette Valley, one of most agriculturally productive regions in the world. This was also a flat section with lots of irrigated fields producing many agricultural products such as seeds and specialty crops. Here, I first saw the fields having water pumped along the road in trenches dug for irrigation purposes. Many western states use this method to enhance the dry climate.

I passed through Salem, Corvallis and Eugene, Oregon, as I headed east. All of these are significant cities, and all are extremely bicycle friendly. Eugene even has a specific bicycle bridge to cross the Willamette River. Fitness stores and bike shops seem to be on every corner. As I rode through this area, the mornings were in the low 40s with afternoon temperatures rising to the 70s. Frequent fog in the morning probably had to do with all the water in the area, but once the sun broke through, I was on the road. I bought sweatpants at Eugene's Goodwill store, just in case it got colder as I climbed.

One motorist evidently didn't like me being on the city streets as I rode into Eugene. He kept passing me as we pulled away from each stoplight. He seemed irritated that I would catch back up again as he came to the next intersection. He yelled out the window, "Why don't you go find a bike path?" I eventually did make a turn that sent me on another street, so I wondered if he was happier then.

Oregon was the most bicycle-friendly state that I rode through. Near Monmouth, I was introduced to a separate lane for cyclists. Such lanes are a big deal for cyclists because traffic is of much less concern. I had not ridden on a full cyclist lane before. Great pavement, well-kept lanes, and no debris or trash of any kind. I understood from locals that the governor and the state government had passed laws to encourage cycling and fitness. Lots of locals were taking advantage of the lane to ride late in the day, but I still only saw a few long-distance cyclists. My only way to define them was if they had heavier bikes fitted with panniers. I soon came to realize that lots of cyclists were out covering long distances while being supported by a van or other vehicle during the day. If they had a flat, help was just a phone call away. Regardless, cyclists of any kind almost always exchanged pleasant words as we passed.

Cross-country cycling or touring is done usually in one of three ways. Totally supported cycling means that there is a vehicle hauling each cyclist's gear, and there is assistance for flats, evening meals, nighttime accommodations, and anything else that is above just riding the bike. I met a group of eight young women headed for Boston using this method, and actually rode near them for three days. They used regular road bikes, which are much easier on the rider, instead of heavier touring bikes like mine. They carried little weight on their lighter bikes, usually only snacks and water. The second method included those groups of cyclists who traveled together and shared tools, food, tents, etc. I saw several of these groups, too, and heard of one with almost 50 people in it. Each cyclist usually carried some of the weight, but total per person weight is limited because the same tent or tool can often be shared by multiple riders. The third and final method was the one I chose. I traveled alone, without any support from others, and carried all the necessary tools and supplies that I may need on the journey.

Traveling alone and carrying my own supplies seemed an easy choice for me. I could set my own schedule without relying on others. It did leave all the decisions, right or wrong, to me alone. I had to live with and deal with any mistakes. Fixing a flat tire was a given. I had to do it, and if I was low on food or water, I had to find some. I will address small groups traveling together in Chapter 5, which is the first time that I began to meet a few westbound TransAmerica cyclists.

Speaking of supplies, I discovered an ongoing education for most of the western half of the country. Since the start of the trip, now nearing 300 miles, supplies were adequate at every turn. If I were running low on water, it wouldn't be long until the next town came within sight. The store owners were all friendly, so it was easy to say, "Do you mind if I fill up my water bottles?" The answer was always a friendly response, something like, "Sure. Go ahead and fill the bottle with ice, too!"

That would change.

My bags were still packed with everything I brought, including my cold-weather supplies. I anticipated that I would need them in Idaho, Montana, Wyoming and Colorado as I went to the higher elevations. I was not carrying much water yet because it wasn't necessary. That would change also, after I learned a harsh lesson.

A week into my ride, I realized that my body was changing slightly. Besides the fact that I was constantly hungry, my arms and shoulders were getting sore and stiff. Years ago, with long-distance running, I learned how important my arms were in helping to provide momentum and strength. On these day-long rides, the quadriceps in my legs carried the load as far as power goes. My arms were used as levers to allow the quads to pump downward while the arms and shoulders held the upper body more rigid. At times, it actually felt like I was pulling against my own arms and shoulders to lever more power to my legs.

As I headed into central Oregon, I found long plateaus to be the norm. The real climbing was beginning, and I knew that soon the elevations would go over 5,000 feet. I celebrated each additional 1,000 feet in altitude. Long and lonely stretches in National Forests would soon teach me how challenging it was to keep food and water available where there were no services accessible.

One humorous event from this area started a trend. At a small, yet adequate, grocery store, I saw huckleberry yogurt and ice cream. I asked a store employee how good huckleberries are, and he said, "You will love it." I bought both the yogurt and ice cream, then soon began a four-state odyssey to get some manner of huckleberry ice cream every time I could find it. I did love the flavor!

I sure had lots to learn, but things were falling slowly into place. I wanted to become an experienced cross-country rider and cut down on mistakes as quickly as possible.

CHAPTER 4
— Eugene to Ochoco Pass, Oregon —

Learning valuable lessons

Oregon is one of the most diverse states on the TransAmerica Trail. I spent several days along the Pacific coast and a few more in the dense forests that support the logging industry. Now it was time to head into the Cascade Mountain Range, one of the most imposing mountain barriers in America. Regular travel across the Cascades did not become commonplace until after gold was discovered in the region. A road was opened to the public in 1862, allowing wagon travel to become possible for prospectors and others heading west.

I spent my first night in the area near McKenzie Bridge. Population centers were close enough that I had no issues finding enough food and other supplies when needed. In many of the towns and crossroads that I would soon begin to encounter, a motel, restaurant and convenience store were often considered extras, yet McKenzie Bridge had one of each and nothing else. McKenzie Bridge was the gateway into the largest climb in Oregon, and a large national park with few services. I loaded up on water and food at the convenience store, and set out to conquer my first major climb.

Cyclists on the TransAmerica have two options for this challenging climb. There is a slightly shorter climb with a higher elevation called McKenzie Pass. On this Saturday, McKenzie Pass was closed to cars and would be hosting a bicycle race. Santiam Pass is longer and the elevation is about 500 feet less. After speaking with the park rangers at their office, I chose the Santiam Pass route. This route is more secluded, making the extra food and water more precious. Built in the 1880s, Santiam Pass allowed fur traders and farmers looking for fertile farmland to head to western Oregon.

There were lots of cyclists in the area, although I found out later that nearly all of them were on hand for the race or for recreational cycling. At this point, I still had seen no confirmed cross-country cyclists. As I was new to my journey, I was unsure of what this day would bring. For several hours, I climbed at a steady pace. Primitive campgrounds and a huge waterfall provided the only scenery. As I climbed higher, I began to notice the lava fields in the area. Lava, or magma, is formed when intense pressure and heat moved large sections of the earth's crust. The material becomes lava when it is pushed through cracks in the earth's surface by gaseous pressures. Lava in this area is dated at about the same time that the Mayflower landed at Plymouth Rock and is easily seen in black piles along the road.

I continued to climb, eventually passing some areas of burned-out forest. Nature uses forest fires to replenish and renew these heavily wooded areas. I realized that I still had about 5-6 miles of climbing and that my water supply was getting low. I found a huge road maintenance facility and used a faucet to refill my bottles. Near that same facility, I spotted two cyclists who were sitting in the shade. They had panniers, meaning that the couple might be long-distance cyclists. The woman surprised me when she said, "Hey mister, do you smoke pot?" I told her no, and then she quickly turned away. Maybe they needed a boost to keep climbing. I never saw them again, and don't know if or how they found the motivation to keep climbing. Within the next mile, I was relegated to pushing the bike as the grade continued to steepen. Balancing the bike is especially hard on slow, uphill grades. My pace had slowed to just above 3 miles an hour as I pedaled in low gear. I could walk with much less effort at 3.6 miles per hour.

Traffic was light as I neared the top. I spotted two things that were welcome sights on these long climbs. Heavy power line towers usually ran along the top of the highest roads. Even better yet was the road sign depicting a steep downhill grade ahead.

My first experience on a fast downhill came on the other side of the summit. The quality of the pavement was great, but I still made sure that my speed didn't exceed 30 mph. Just a little pothole or bad place in the road can topple a rider and end a good day, so I was cautious with this first encounter of long downhill. Total coasting length was about 5 miles and then the road mostly flattened out as I headed toward Sisters, a trendy small town whose landscape is dominated by three snow-capped mountains. The long flat stretch took me right into Sisters late in the afternoon. I stopped to reload at a nice convenience store, and made a few calls about possible motels in the area. "Trendy" in this case meant that the motel prices were out of my price range, one of only two times that I was quoted a nightly rate of close to $150. My next move, and one that served me well later in the trip, was to call the local bike shop for a suggestion. He said, "If you have energy left, ride on to Redmond. The motel prices are much better and there is a bigger selection."

A huge coincidence of my stop at that convenience store was another encounter with one of the park rangers that I had met while asking for information on the Santiam Pass area. I was now almost 50 miles away from her office, and she was standing next to me in line. She said, "You made it!" That was a nice moment.

I called the Motel Redmond, got directions and a great cyclist's price, and headed that way. Most of the ride was fueled by a tailwind pushed toward me off a nearby thunderstorm. With the tailwind, and my renewed energy, I rode 20 miles in less than an hour and a half. The motel manager even helped me carry my bike upstairs. I catalogued the idea of calling bike shops for advice.

At the end of the day, I had a major revelation about my ability to complete the cross-country journey. There was no doubt in my mind now that I could do it! With a major climb and a long ride of 79 miles that day, I was bolstered with new-found confidence. Then I experienced a yearning for ice cream. This was the first night that I got ice cream as a part of my evening meal. It was an immediate pick-me-up, so I knew I'd be seeking out ice cream from that day forward.

I had ridden into an area of Oregon that began to look like the Old Wild West. My elevation was still close to 3,000 feet and the landscape was becoming more arid. I headed toward Prineville, near the geographical center of Oregon and also the only city in the United States that has built and operates its own rail line. The next major challenge was Ochoco Pass, another peak just below 5,000 feet. It was not as steep as the Santiam, but would take close to 20 miles of steady climbing to get over it. This was the first hot day of my journey, and I made sure to load up on plenty of water. Ochoco Pass was situated in the middle of a genuine wilderness area, and I was about to learn a valuable lesson.

As the temperature continued to rise and the climbing grade worsened, I kept pushing forward. This area was one of the less scenic of the trip so far. Lots of trees and not much else made for a boring ride. I started to use up my water, and actually ran out with about 6 miles to go before reaching the peak. Shortly, the danger level would increase without some additional water. Signs for a rest area ahead gave me hope that I could get water there. At first sight, I realized that there was not potable water because the bathrooms were porta-johns. Luckily for me, a surveyor was working in the area and had plenty of water, but only because he had exchanged trucks with a co-worker. After he gave me a couple of bottles, I vowed not to be caught lacking again. This was the first time that I was dehydrated and out of water. My energy had faded quickly and I was just short of being in real trouble. I swallowed the first bottle of water in one long gulp and then savored the second. Up and over the pass I went.

CHAPTER 5
— Mitchell to Coburg, Oregon —

Finding confidence in my climbing

My daylong target destination had been a little town called Mitchell. It came after the long downhill ride from the Ochoco Pass and then a steady climb into the town. According to my map, Mitchell had all services, so I expected food and plenty of options. I was whipped at the end of my ride, but confidently rode into town with great expectations. I stopped quickly and walked into an old-time neighborhood general store. The owner said, "If you want something, you better get it in the next 15 minutes, because we are about to close." I asked about the cafés, and learned that one didn't open that day and the other was closed. So, I got some ice cream and Pop-Tarts and went to check on a room. The local hotel had a room but I would share a bathroom with at least five other people. It was essentially a hostel room with too many people sharing the same bathroom. There was a motel up on the highway, one that didn't look to have any business. I called and booked a high-priced room and went back to get more ice cream just as the general store closed.

Maybe all this had to do with Mitchell's past. Mitchell had an early history of dealing with serious floods in 1884 and 1904. At least two major fires also damaged the small town in 1896 and 1899. For many years, it was the central trading post for ranchers and miners. No doubt, the little town was going to be visited by every passing cyclist, yet supplies were hard to come by in this area.

I mentioned earlier that I had not seen other cross-country cyclists. I found three in Mitchell: one from California had arrived just after me to join two Scandinavians who were already camping in the town park. All were headed east. The cyclist from California said he had started just a few days before at an alternative point. He didn't ride the coast like I did, but began his journey about 300 miles later. We talked briefly and then I left to go to the motel. I never saw them again. This was a tough 70-mile day, with heat being a part of the equation. I did enjoy a mountaintop view of the whole area that evening as the sun went down on one of the most interesting and challenging days of my first two weeks on the road.

Cellphone coverage had been limited all day and would continue to be sporadic at best for the next three weeks. Verizon was not the carrier of choice for the locals, and I was warned to not expect regular service until I hit eastern Colorado.

I was on the road early the next morning. The climbing started quickly and I worked hard to get over Keye's Pass. Few vehicles were on the road, making for a pleasant struggle — if there can be such a thing. Mornings were cool throughout Oregon, and the sun rose early as we were quickly approaching the longest days of the year. My water bottles were full, and my focus was on Dayville, Oregon, listed as 40 miles away, but reportedly with several stores that I desperately needed to visit.

I made the summit and rode a steady downhill into Dayville. I had completed those 40 miles before 10:30 a.m., and needed a good breakfast. Dayville was a stop on the old stagecoach line, squarely in the middle of some beautiful ranching country. As I rode through, hay was being harvested and loaded on trucks. Fossil research is also ongoing in the area, providing an interesting look into America's past.

When I hit town, I had one plan: to get a good breakfast! Plenty of ice water, an omelet and pancakes made for the perfect breakfast at the Dayville Cafe. Ice water is hard to beat, especially with a couple of good slices of lemon. The waitress filled me in on other cyclists who had passed by in the last few days. I counted this as the best breakfast on the whole trip. When planning my long-distance adventure, I thought regular breakfasts be would part of my daily journey. However, I found that the best time to get a jump on the day was early in the morning and those cooler hours were less dehydrating. The ability to find a restaurant during mid-morning hours was much harder than I thought, so breakfasts became only an occasional treat.

After leaving the café, I went across the street to get some food for later. What I didn't expect was a lecture on how few cyclists realize that they were now in the wilderness. The owner didn't think we took enough precautions to ensure safety. She also didn't like the idea of women traveling across the country alone or without men. I can remember only one woman, who I met much later, that was traveling alone. I headed out for another long ride to the next town.

My goal was Prairie City, another old west town. Most of the day, I had a good tailwind and the riding was easier than some previous days. I began to think that another mantra for the ride might be, "Never waste a tailwind!" Tailwinds provide a mental lift that transcends the body. The extra pushing force generated by Mother Nature is next in line as the best gift to a rider, just behind the relative desired safety associated with such an adventurous trip. My best advice for the day came at a stop at the John Day Dairy Queen late in the afternoon. The young women there told me that I could use Prairie City for a quick start toward climbing three more high passes that would come in a quick 20-mile segment. The smiles and the ice cream that they provided carried me to Prairie City in a flash.

I felt like I was riding into history upon entering Prairie City, the early mining and livestock center for the valley. Main Street still listed lots of interesting sites, including the Historic Hotel Prairie. My room that night was probably once used by a gunslinger with a need to even a score. Thoroughly restored way beyond any means that I required, I loved it. The manager even helped me to get my bike into the room. Prairie City had a laundromat and I washed all my cycling clothes while enjoying a wonderful sourdough grilled cheese sandwich. Mechanically, I had done pretty well so far, but getting one of those washing machines and a dryer to work was a big challenge for me.

The morning dawned and I had the expectation of climbing those three high peaks in rapid succession. I was now traveling in what is known as the high desert. All three peaks had steep climbs to over 5,000 feet, then descended slightly before the next climb. Adding to the mix was the fact that there were no supplies available for 68 miles. After loading my bags with lots of water, I headed out of town and immediately up the first climb. Plenty of gulches, draws and passes were going to make up this long day. It seemed as if I was climbing every mountain possible.

The three passes went on and on, making sure I sharpened my climbing skills. I kept the wheels turning and remembered the caution from the hotel manager that there would be actually another climb after the three passes were completed. I dealt with my hardest day yet. The mountains were getting higher and more numerous and the altitude was significant, which probably was a factor in my labored breathing. Much warmer daytime temperatures became my regular companion.

Baker City, Oregon, was the expected destination for this challenging day. Baker City was another gold boom town that still seems to be doing quite well. An 84-ounce gold nugget was once found nearby. Large grazing areas filled with tumbleweed plants dominated the landscape. A long downhill and flat ride on good roads helped compensate for a headwind and steady rain during the afternoon. I had spent the whole ride so far in Oregon, but would soon head into Idaho.

I mentioned in Chapter 3 that I would address the advantage in traveling in groups on a long and challenging cycling trip. Since Mitchell, I had met no other eastbound cyclists. Interesting was the fact that I met several groups of westbound cyclists and two others who were traveling on their own. All of these groups had a member or two who had left them over a disagreement, and one of the single cyclists was now riding along with the use of maps that he copied with his phone. When I asked why he didn't have his own maps, he replied that his best friend had left him and taken their maps. The best friend said the ride was too hard and that he was going home. However, cyclists of like mind often seemed to match up and ride for long stretches together after they met on the road. Spending 24 hours a day together, complete with the stress of decisions and physical challenges, was not easy. The result of discussions that I had with other cyclists was that groups were great, but only if the dynamic was right. When it is, then the ride could possibly be easier on all involved. If not, nothing could replace the freedom of mind and spirit that could be lost and result in the long adventure being less enjoyable than it should be.

CHAPTER 6
— Baker City, Oregon to Cambridge, Idaho —

My first new state, and a new time zone

Rain was falling in a steady drizzle when I checked out of my hotel in Baker City, Oregon. Threatening clouds confirmed the forecast of an increasing cold rain as the day wore on. The desk clerk told me that two other cyclists were staying put for the day. They had checked in later than me, so I had no idea who they were. I was committed to rolling on. My Tyvek rain jacket had proved its worth during the rainy days along the Pacific.

For me, staying off the road for any amount of time due to a moderate rain would be a mistake. Rain was OK to ride in because the fenders on the Surly bike were keeping it off me from underneath. Both panniers were waterproof and only my backpack was going to soak up any moisture. A cold rain was a different story, especially if wind was involved.

I put my wallet and iPad in the panniers and rode to another great find on the way out of town. Safeway grocery stores have everything, including a huge choice on energy bars and pastries. I had begun to favor early-morning pastries as a quick breakfast food with an energy charge. The clerk told me that I could save a lot of money by getting a Safeway card, so I did. This proved to be another bright move as I was able to use it in various grocery stores as far away as South Carolina. Safeway is owned by Kroger and so are lots of other chains, and that card worked in all of them.

While standing underneath the overhang outside the store and downing my food, I thought that this would be a great chance to verify my directions for heading out of town. A man in a big Suburban watched me eat, so I asked him if Cedar Street was close by.

He seemed a little wary and rolled his window up a little before answering, "That is it right across from the grocery store." I didn't want a ride, just good directions.

The rain was picking up, and although Baker City had been nice, it was time to roll on. This was my 10th day on the road and I had covered 600 miles. All of it was in Oregon, and I was definitely ready to try out a new state. Soon, I would get that chance. I left Baker City and almost immediately climbed Flagstaff Hill with good energy. It was long enough to get my attention, though, as the rain started to fall heavily, and was soon joined by a sporadic headwind. The scenery was full of more tumbleweed grazing areas. No wonder these cows required so many acres to graze on. There is little grass for them to eat and I have wondered if the cows ever chose to eat the tumbleweeds.

As the wind increased, I was fortunate to join up with the Powder River as it flowed downstream. Throughout my journey, I learned a lot about rivers and how they influence the difficulty of the ride. In this case, the Powder River was steadily running downhill while making turns left and right. A river running downstream is good news for the cyclist, because the grade is generally downhill, too. Sometimes, there would be rolling hills where the engineers chose to pave over the rises in grade that accompany the valley terrain. This happened on the lesser roads usually. Yet, it was always good to see a downstream-running river flowing in my direction. If the river ran with some whitewater, then the cyclist was going to scoot downhill pretty fast. A fast-running river with whitewater usually meant a shorter downhill ride than that of a gently moving one. Upstream rivers had their own set of issues, the foremost of which was the uphill grade. When riding against a gently flowing river, especially if wind was not an issue, this ride could be fairly pleasant, too. Often, the middle gears handled the climb well and the slightly slower pace allowed for more time to view the scenery. The worst river of all is the river that pounds and roars down toward you, splashing water loud enough to hear. Low gears are required for the duration of the time that the cyclist climbs upstream. Luckily, I didn't have many long rides upstream along these fast-moving rivers.

The Powder River was my ace in the hole today. The rain and wind had joined with the cold to make the day miserable. There was little interesting scenery and I began to think of possibly ending the day early as I got colder. My plan was to let weather conditions dictate days off, and although I would still get a significant amount of mileage today, the thought of spending the afternoon in front of a heater had become more inviting. Not surprisingly, I was really hungry, too.

First things first. I had to pedal through the town of Richland on the way to yet another climb. I stopped at the general store and grabbed two must-haves. I bought a pair of heavy insulated gloves and a couple of double packs of Reese's Cups. The store clerk told me that my next stop should be for a hot cup of coffee in the café next door. We discussed the impending climb after I declined the offer, and she showed me the mountain out her front window. "It's not all that steep, but it is a steady 4½-mile climb that does not let up. Once you make the other side, the downhill will provide a good boost," the clerk said.

I had learned to take descriptions of climbing grades from non-cyclists with my eyes wide open. The clerk said the climb was not steep, but she was used to seeing it from a car. She hadn't had the pleasure of trying to balance the bike in granny gear while moving painfully and persistently slowly toward an always hidden summit. I would think, "Is the next turn the one that brings me to the top?" More often than not, the disappointment of yet another series of switchbacks would signal more climbing. I was now experienced enough to watch for how and where the power wires crossed the summit.

My new gloves helped get feeling to return to my fingers as I left

27

the store, my energy recharged on the peanut butter cups. The rain was still coming down, but I didn't feel the wind as much. One of the few advantages of climbing when there is a headwind around is that the headwind might be blocked by the mountain. This appeared to be the case, and held true as I climbed one of the steepest grades yet on the trip. I'm sure it was not too bad in a car, but finally I did reach the top and looked forward to that rewarding downhill. This mountain didn't even have a name, even though most of the western mountain passes did.

Just as I expected, the other side of the pass held the brunt of the wind. To my advantage, the wind was now strong from my left. I would take a side wind over a head wind anytime, but I soon learned how dangerous side winds can be. As I coasted down the other side of the mountain, strong gusts came from my left and pushed the bike sideways. If I didn't shift my weight quickly, I could be blown over or off the road. Several times while descending, I was blown dangerously close to the edge of the road. There was little traffic, so my plan was to stay near the center lane until a vehicle came. This ride down was one of the few times that I was actually scared of what the wind could do. Finally at the bottom of the hill, I relaxed and followed the signs on into Halfway.

I had spent most of the day riding along the famous Oregon Trail, originally 2,000 miles long and established by a company headed by John Jacob Astor. Beginning in 1842, hundreds of wagon trains headed west on that famous trail. In many places, you can still see deep ruts made by the wagons.

I was cold enough to give it up for the rest of the afternoon. My shoes and socks were soaked, and the cold wind on the downhill ride had chilled me even worse than before. My hands remained warm, and I was thankful. Today's journey had been through an area called Hell's Canyon. The name was a good fit. I got a great deal on a motel in Halfway, and by 2 p.m. was well settled in front of a heater. Halfway is small, but had two good grocery stores. I chose one and bought a bunch of microwaveable vegetables, some produce, yogurt and cookies and headed back to the room to stay warm and listen to the rain fall. It was a restful night.

I was out early the next morning into a much lighter drizzle and breeze, heading east toward another big climb over another pass. I was excited that today would be the day that I crossed into Idaho, and also left the Pacific Time Zone by cycling into the Mountain Time Zone. It would be hard to leave Oregon, a state with no sales tax, plenty of great scenery and a love for cyclists. But it was time to go to Idaho.

My first 20 miles heading east that morning brought me into improving weather. I was back into Hell's Canyon and enjoying the scenery. My route followed the road to the Brownlee Dam and Reservoir and as soon as I turned right, the grade was steep and a headwind building. The road eventually leveled out some, and as I started riding along the reservoir, the headwind was strong enough to be pushing the water past me. For some reason, the pedaling was hard, even harder than I thought the wind should make it. I looked down and realized that my front tire was going flat. This was my 11th day and I was going to have my first flat tire. I pulled over to a beautiful spot beside the water and started to empty my panniers. My tools and spare tubes were in the bottom of the bags. In all my days of riding a bike, mostly of the mountain variety, I had never needed to fix a flat tire. I simply sat down and prayed that I could make the repair and keep going. This was a fairly secluded spot, though I could walk to a campground or the dam if I had to. I had received a gift of CO2 cartridges from a former girlfriend, one of several tools that I used on the trip. The tire appeared to stop losing air after I took the weight off it, so I took the cartridge and quickly pumped up the tire, not really expecting it to work. Amazingly — and I am still shaking my head at this — the tire did seem to hold. Just then, a couple of TransAmerica cyclists heading west rode up, the first cyclists I had seen in two days. We talked a little about their experiences with flats, and they spoke of regular issues with flat tires and broken spokes. The tire continued to hold, and I reloaded my bags and tools. We shared more information on what to expect over the next few days.

The Idaho state line sign came into view just as I was riding past the dam. As would become my custom, I stopped and made a photo of the sign. Two fishermen photographed me as I stood with my bike. I had now completed one time zone and one long state. I forged ahead into Idaho and spent most of the rest of the day climbing another nameless pass. Wind was once again an issue as I pushed to the top, and some of those winds were forcing me sideways as well as backward. I took pushing breaks, but was able to get back on to ride over the summit. Another magical and amazing thing happened! The wind on the other side of the mountain was a strong tailwind. Only a few times did this happen to me on the entire cross-country trip, but I was thankful each time it did. I coasted almost all the way down to one of my favorite little towns, Cambridge, Idaho. It was easy for me to love the little towns that didn't require climbing a hill to enter the town.

Cambridge was a friendly town, with just about everything I needed. I stopped at a bike/book shop just as they were about to close. The store owner had to call the bike repair guy back to the store, but she said he wouldn't mind at all. Dinah was the owner and Tom Lund responded quickly to her call. Before she left, Dinah set me up with an acceptable rate at one of the local motels. Tom arrived and checked out the bike, and especially the front tire. He could find nothing wrong and I felt good that the tube would hold. Tom wouldn't take any money for what he did, saying, "I just want to see you guys keep moving safely on your journey." I thanked Tom profusely and headed for my motel. Rozita Bailey was another of those remarkably friendly people who met me at the front desk as I entered the Frontier Motel. She knew I was coming and had already set me up in a great room that would also hold my bike. This would end another challenging day with a total of only 60 miles, yet it was enough for this day. I was learning that one 60-mile day was probably not going to be the same as another.

I walked down the street and ordered some food from the diner and then continued over to the grocery store to get some more food. The checkout clerk invited me to a community celebration that was being held in the park. There was free barbecue, and although I am a vegetarian, I considered going to see if I could make a meal off the fixings. Later that evening as I sat outside submitting my newspaper story for the day, the same clerk from the store stopped by the motel and asked if I had enjoyed the barbecue. These were some special people. The mountain range around Cambridge was so spectacular that I remained outside almost until dark.

Today, I had left behind Oregon, the Oregon Trail and the Snake River Canyon. The Snake River Canyon is often one of the hottest canyons in Oregon and Idaho. My luck held as I visited it on a cool day; however, the same headwind that made it cool pushed me backward on the long climb. There seems always to be a trade-off.

Tomorrow, there would be yet another big mountain to climb. Different about this mountain was that it was a gradual climb and the downhill would be the same. I had high hopes for a good day tomorrow as I drifted off to another peaceful sleep. The daily physical challenge was building, but my confidence was, too. I felt good about each day and fell asleep each night when my head hit the pillow. As the journey developed, my sleep improved. I knew my need for sleep was increasing, and my commitment to getting that sleep had to follow along.

CHAPTER 7
— Cambridge, Idaho to the Montana State Line —

Mixing climbing with history

I headed east once again the next morning, more rested than I had been since the first day of the journey. It was still cloudy and cool as I began the long climb to an area called New Meadows. The steep segments were short, but the grade was relentless. I leap-frogged often with a group of eastbound cyclists, a young couple and two young women who had recently joined them. One of the women was one of the best climbers that I had seen, proven by her constantly catching and passing the rest of her group and me on the uphills. Eventually, the long, tree-lined climb broke out into a flat stretch of road that led into town. It had taken me until 2:30 p.m. to cover the 48 miles of climbing that day. Total time was over seven hours. I was out of energy and stopped in at a Subway to eat and check messages on WiFi. My progress during the morning was slow and somewhat disappointing. It became a low mark for the rest of the week. From that time forward, I wanted to make sure that more miles were covered by 2:30 p.m. Armed with a bag of Subway oatmeal raisin cookies, I was back on the road again to another pleasant surprise.

Leaving New Meadows, I turned onto a new section of Highway 95. It had all the things I wanted so that I could pick up the pace as the afternoon proceeded. There was a great bike lane beside the highway, plus there was beautiful scenery as I looked over large ranches and beautiful snow-covered mountain ranges behind them. The grade was mostly flat and a slight tailwind had developed. All of these factors added up to a much faster pace as I pushed toward my destination of Riggins, Idaho.

I began following the Little Salmon River on a steady downhill, with a special twist for later that afternoon. The Little Salmon is one of those rivers that takes a fast pace, so it allowed me to follow along with little pedaling effort. Rain was falling again, but I didn't care. A steady headwind couldn't hold back my progress on the enjoyable ride toward Riggins. The depth of the surrounding canyon grew higher as the road continued to follow the river. As I neared town, cars and trucks lined both sides of the road along the river and I wondered why. Locals told me later that the salmon were running and this was a big event for residents.

Riggins is yet another gold boom town. The first gold strikes were made in 1860 and soon, prospectors flooded the area. While searching for a motel to spend the night, I noticed that Riggins had some of the most dramatic scenery yet. Good motel prices but poor WiFi reception dictated my choice that evening. I sat outside and watched the fading light change the colors on the high hills that enveloped Main Street. I chose a motel that is included on the National Historical Register because a returning GI from World War II had a grand idea. He thought that there would be a big need for motels after the war, and built a large series of small cabins. I got one of them, but was disappointed to find that my bike was not allowed in the room. This was the only motel on my whole trip that did not allow the bikes inside even though they were easily accessible. Other places wouldn't have decent inside access, but I always found a reasonable way to get the bike close by.

Gold was not the only economic magnet that attracted whites to this area of eastern Oregon. Tributaries that empty into the nearby Powder River were among the gold hot spots, but additionally miners found lodes of copper, silver and other valuable minerals throughout this region. As I rode east the next morning, I began to notice that a lot of closed mines were clearly visible along the roadside. I wondered what might have transpired behind those now closed doors. Signs of "Mine — Keep Out" just made me want to

33

take a look inside even more.

This morning's ride continued along the Salmon River, easy and fast to begin with. On the west side of the river were sites of many past mines including a few that still showed signs of activity. The valley continued to deepen as I headed into the White Bird Valley. The elevation had fallen to just below 2,000 feet and I knew that another climb would be the result. My first entrance into an Indian Reservation was about to occur, and I had been tipped off that these areas had spectacular scenery but few services. They were also loaded with history.

The influx of livestock growers, miners and settlers eventually destroyed the peaceful existence between the Indians and whites. As hard feelings developed between the two sides, pressure was put on the government to set aside land for just the Indians and other land for the whites. The Indians saw this concept as unthinkable, expecting one person or segment of that person's group to have the ability to control land. In 1877, the Nez Perce Indians, led by Chief Joseph, agreed to leave their homeland and travel to a reservation. Just before that move was to take place, three young braves attacked white settlers. They killed three and wounded three more. Chief Joseph was shocked by their actions but still hoped to avoid war. The settlers appealed to the U.S. Army for protection. When Captain Perry and the soldiers entered the area, they found that Joseph and the Nez Perce had moved to the White Bird area. Perry's men fired on a Nez Perce truce party, setting off a short but decisive battle. The Indians used their old weapons and knowledge of the area to soundly defeat the troops. The Nez Perce war had officially begun.

Large parts of my riding over the next few days would be along many of the historical sites of the Nez Perce war. I confess to having known very little about this history before I rode into the area, but was soon amazed at how the Indians did their best to avoid war and how the US government mishandled the situation time and again. The first 20 miles of the ride toward White Bird passed quickly. I confidently followed my maps into the small town and saw the highway quickly pass above me. There was one store open and thankfully it had some of the supplies that I needed, plus some Reese's Cups to help energize my mountain climb. I asked the lady who ran the store for her advice on the coming climb. Once more I heard the dreaded, "It is long but not very steep. It used to be the old highway to the next town, but now it slowly climbs up to join the new highway that you just left. It is an easier climb because it has lots of switchbacks."

I rode away and headed east out of town hoping, but not expecting, an easy climb. She was right about the first part as I left the town and passed a few small ranches. It was easy enough, but I saw the same road winding back and forth way ahead on a steep looking mountain. Soon the road started to become steeper and it crossed a cattle guard in the road. Cattle guards are rows of pipes that cars can drive over but cows won't cross. Bikes have to be walked over them, too. Eventually, the road started to wind round and round the mountain, passing cows that were on open range grazing. No fences were in sight and the cows had pooped often right in the road as they wandered to another section of grass. The rancher happened to be out working the cows and moving all of them downhill, then eventually onto a trailer. He left a forlorn bull there who just keep watching me and wondering if I had anything to do with his harem leaving.

Just before cresting the mountain, I missed a turn to the right, but realized that I could reintersect quickly by going ahead on the same road. There was a short downhill and then a pleasant and mostly flat ride into Grainger, Idaho. I stopped at one convenience store and got a few things to eat, since all of this climbing had once again made me hungry. I asked the clerk how far to Kooskia, my destination for the night. She sourly replied, "I don't know, I have never been there and couldn't give you an idea." I rode on and within a mile I stopped again at another convenience store to ask again. The clerk was interested in my ride and we had a nice conversation. She said, "Oh, it is only about 17 more miles and the terrain is reasonable. Plus you will love the town." I didn't buy a thing but knew it wouldn't have mattered to this woman. I smiled as I rode away, thinking about the difference in the two clerks.

The terrain was rolling, back into the farming and ranching country briefly, before joining the Clearwater River as it gently flowed downhill into Kooskia. I remember this late-afternoon ride as one of my most pleasant. It was beautifully scenic, dotted with historical markers from the Nez Perce War, and downhill on a comfortably warm day. Late in the day, I rolled into another of my favorite small towns in America.

Main Street and lots of older buildings dominate Kooskia, like much of small-town America. I thought I was set with a pre-arranged motel reservation, but I rode on through the town without finding the motel. I stopped and was standing on Main Street with a look of bewilderment when a local resident pulled up to ask if I needed help. I told him that I was sure I had a motel room, but didn't see the motel. The resident said he wasn't familiar with that particular motel either, so I was afraid that I had called another town on the map by mistake. The same resident offered to go back to the middle of the town and help me figure it out, so I followed him on my bike. We realized that the name of the motel was incorrect on my map, and he sent me with good wishes toward the motel office. Thus began one of the most interesting motel visits of the 54 days on the road.

I stopped in the office and the manager came out as expected. I told her that I had a reservation, but she didn't think so. Then I told her the rate, and she said, "That's right!", so I started to feel OK. The manager apologized and got me set up in a room, but told me that the room wasn't quite ready yet. I quickly realized that this lady was overworked as she headed off to finish up the room, apologizing for the oversight as she went. Kooskia has at least a couple of good restaurants, a great grocery store, and lots more. My thoughts turned to a laundromat, and I asked whether there was one. The motel manager said, "How many pieces do you have?" and I answered five. She said, "I will wash them with some other things that I am doing." We began to talk and I found that she had worked in various parts of the country and even in London, and was now working at the motel in hopes of building her own house. Not only did she want her own house, but she wanted to get off the grid. "Getting off the grid" means away from most others, only coming to civilization when needed, and being invisible to the government.

My clothes arrived about an hour later, totally clean and smelling good for probably the first time in close to a week. We talked some more, and realized that the largest full moon of the year was due in just over an hour. I went off to grab something to eat at both the café and grocery store. In yet another special coincidence, the same resident who helped me find the motel was at the deli counter. We introduced ourselves and he told me of a desire to walk across part of California to honor his dad. I came back to find the motel manager out looking at the moon as it rose. I hoped that things will work out well for her. As I went to bed that night, it occurred to me how interesting some of the people are and that they are the real focus of the trip. Challenges, discovery and meeting lots of good people — that is why I was out there on my cross-country trip.

Kooskia was my launching pad for the biggest climb so far. I would spend about 80 miles climbing steadily toward the top of Lolo Pass. Lolo was used by the Nez Perce as they began a trip toward Canada trying to escape the U.S. troops. They used an old Indian trail called the Lolo Trail for a forced march that could potentially total 1,300 miles.

The Lewis and Clark Expedition also spent extensive time in this area and called it "the most formidable barrier of our entire journey." A half century later, it was called the "most difficult and uninviting country" by an expedition from the U.S. Department of the Interior. My own issue was that this climb would extend for more than 65 miles without any chance of resupply. As I rolled into the area, I found the road being repaved and was stripped down to a rough grid. There was no choice but to ride slowly and limit the vibration. My plan was to stop for breakfast on this morning, and get fortified for the long climb. The first restaurant that I stopped at was just opening and was serving buffet style. I was met at the door and told that the buffet was $10 and would include no pancakes or waffles. The waitress said quietly, "About four miles on down the road, you will find a restaurant that you will like better." I smiled and took her advice and headed to the other restaurant.

After good pancakes and eggs, I stopped at the general store next door and got a few more things to eat later. The clerk told me that the climb wasn't too bad, so my red flag went up. My bags were full and off I rode beside the Lochsa River, heading upstream. For more than 40 miles, I steadily rode uphill in fourth gear. The clerk was right, and I kept pushing until reaching one of the densest forests yet. A well placed ranger station provided fresh water and a short break for my legs. My goal was to make it to within a few miles of the summit and camp at the first sign of civilization. That spot was the Lochsa Lodge, a small site with a general store, restaurant, cabins and free camping for cyclists. After 93 long and challenging miles, I was totally used up as I set up my campsite. Light rain was falling and I couldn't wait to fill my stomach and head for bed. A good meal at the restaurant and plenty of snacks from the store did the job and I was asleep as quickly as my head hit the sleeping bag.

Next morning was another story. Light rain had fallen all night and my tent had begun to leak. I kicked myself for buying a cheap tent just because it was very light. After packing up and loading the bike, I resolved to get a new tent at the first opportunity. My front tire was again slowly leaking air, so I pumped it up and vowed to address that soon, too. For some reason, I didn't feel optimistic about the day. The general store clerk told me that the top of the pass was 10 miles away. After more than 11 miles, I topped that sucker and reached the state of Montana for the first time, another challenge completed. This was the first time that people thought I looked bad as I climbed. Two motorists stopped to ask if I needed anything. This one was hard because of the length of the climb. I already knew from others that the downhill would be long and on good roads. I couldn't wait to see what Montana had to offer.

CHAPTER 8
— Lolo, Montana to Dillon, Montana —

More climbing as I head for the national parks

I had settled into the ride. I had learned a lot already that would improve the next 3,000 miles. Most of the gear had been exactly what I needed; therefore, I was not carrying extra weight. My confidence continued to build with a resolve that I could handle the issues that might arise. No part of my body seemed to be in distress, except that my stomach never had quite enough to be content. In this chapter, I will talk about my bike, my gear and my body as they dealt with the stress of even higher mountains and longer days.

It was time for more climbing. I headed through the heart of the big sky country, one of the most beautiful states along the TransAmerica Trail. I knew I would encounter even more spectacular scenery.

My first night in Montana was in Hamilton, located in the Bitterroot Range of the Rockies. Explorers Lewis and Clark were given credit as being the first white men in the valley. All of the Bitterroot Valley was once part of a giant lake, but is now used for hay and ranch land. My feet and legs were tired and I didn't smell the best, but I chose to eat and write my journal entry before the shower.

My stomach had begun to empty really fast, so tonight I gave it some attention. I had already had a small pizza and an order of breadsticks. I quickly downed a quart of yogurt, followed by some cookies and bananas. I inhaled power bars later. I had developed a pattern that included a rich carbohydrate breakfast and snacks throughout the day. Stopping for full meals didn't seem to be worth wasting my time. My morning energy seemed better and my best days equated to an early start and at least 40 miles by noon. I had never eaten 4,000-5,000 calories regularly at an evening meal before, but it sure was easy now. Eating late and plentiful was my plan.

I developed another habit. If I stayed in a motel and had a good TV, my first choice in shows would be old Westerns. Watching Westerns on TV or at the movies had always been fun for me. Now that I had seen the same scenery, it was fun to watch the story but look past the main characters and see if a mountain, gulch, pass or draw looked familiar. Additionally, I looked for rodeos. Every town in the West has a rodeo at some time of the year, or so it appeared. I resolved to see if I could match an afternoon or overnight stay with a weekend rodeo. Being in the Wild West was just plain fun! (But only when there was plenty of food available.)

Another hard climb loomed. I knew that this one would be especially long too, but the TransAmerica maps gave cross-country cyclists two alternates. Once again, one was higher and steeper and the other was just slightly less in elevation but on a gravel road instead of pavement. My plan was to stop and see the rangers just before making the choice. But first, I had to get out of town.

There was a bike shop in Hamilton, but, like most, this one didn't open early and I didn't want to wait around. The front tire was still slowly leaking, but a good air compressor would bring it back to speed quickly. First stop after leaving the motel was a gas station with an air hose in front. I pulled up to it and a guy walked around the corner to tell me there was no air. I said, "I just need a little. When will it be up?" He replied, "I am working on the compressor now, but about three blocks farther down the street is another station." So, I walked the bike to that store. Once again, a free air hose was hanging from the back of the store. I couldn't get it to work and asked the clerk inside. He came out and got it working, and soon I was ready to roll. All I needed was air and Reese's Cups. It was one of the few mornings that I had not yet found my usual energy and I didn't know why. Out of town I rolled on a long and flat street.

At the city limits, the flatness turned quickly into an uphill grade and continued all the way to Darby, Montana. An unusual morning headwind pushed me backward. In the closing chapters, I will make a list of the top 10 small towns on my journey. Darby will make that list. After 16 challenging miles, I passed a rodeo about to start. Rodeos don't usually happen on a weekday morning, and most curious was that this one was going to be huge. About that time, I saw the Montana Café and decided that a good breakfast was the perfect ticket. It certainly couldn't hurt. Darby had lots of small shops and a couple of other restaurants, but it was a real treat to stop at this one. One large family ran the Montana Café. Mom and Dad, the grandparents on one side and plenty of kids were doing a great job. I got another satisfying order of pancakes and eggs and enjoyed talking with one of the sons, who served as my waiter. His asked thoughtful questions about my ride, and soon I was visiting with the whole family. They told me that the rodeo was some type of big masters championship, meaning that older cowboys were competing. The café family loaded me up on chocolate chip cookies and I pedaled out of town toward the big climb, only a time or two thinking of turning back to watch some of the rodeo.

Leaving Darby, I met a couple of female cyclists who were working on a flat tire. They told me that eight young women were riding a route that would take them to Boston from Seattle, and a van was supporting them. They had the situation well in hand and I rode on, beginning a leap-frog routine with these ladies for the next three days. They were all in their early 20s, lively and supportive of me. Every time the van would ride by with water and snacks for them, they offered me something, too. These women all rode light road bikes and let the van haul their equipment, so their pace was quick. Their official title was the Cycle Co-Op Girls.

Just out of Darby, and past a last convenience store and ice cream sandwich, I headed for the ranger station. After a short talk with one of the helpful and attractive women who worked in the office, and a chance to see pictures of the dirt road, I headed for what was this time supposed to be the shorter route over the mountain. The first part of the ride was a gentle climb, but it began to rise more quickly than the paved alternative. How did I know? Because I was above the paved road and looked down on it during miles of climbing. Heavy rocks, the size of my foot, were all over the road, and I was forced to walk because of them. Soon there were so many that I could barely push the bike and hold it up straight as we both bounced over the rocks. After close to 10 miles of little riding and lots of pushing, I finally crested the pass and hoped for a quick downhill. Being on a dirt road with little road maintenance, I was soon riding a washboard. Little ridges in the road had replaced the big rocks and every time I got any speed going the ridges in the road forced me to slow down. Once more I had chosen to take the alternate and my resolve stiffened to make it be the last time.

Once back on the main road, a gentle downhill made a pleasant ride on a good road toward Wisdom, Montana. The Co-Op Girls soon appeared and passed me as they headed for Wisdom, too. Montana is called the Big Sky Country, and I believe the name comes because it is easy to see for many miles in any direction. We passed a National Monument for another Nez Perce battlefield. This time, the soldiers attacked the sleeping Indian camp at dawn. The Indians once again outfought the soldiers and held them at bay for two days. Past the battlefield, I hung on to the sight of the last two women and followed on into town. I could see the early evening lights of the town for miles out and wondered if I would have enough energy to get there. The Co-Op Girls were going to camp in the town park in the rain, and asked if I wanted to join them. This time I had a motel, the only one in a town with a listed population of 119. We parted company after they made sure I had plenty of food for the evening.

I quickly checked into the motel and asked about my favorite subject again. Food! It was on my mind more and more. The motel owner told me that there were two saloons in town and both had bar food. The general store was closed and would reopen the next morning. So, I picked a saloon and walked over for their first-ever veggie sub and some chips. I had plenty of water, cookies and brownies in my bags. My evening menu was quickly set. I slept well that night while listening to another gentle rain.

First thing next morning, I was ready to roll with my raincoat on. I stopped in the local tractor shop for front tire air and waited for the compressor to build up. Just across the street was the general store. There were just enough items to load my bags again. Reese's Cups on top! Across the country, I never found a single store that didn't carry Reese's Cups. I got my air and headed out toward the day's climb, another long and mostly gentle one. A slight headwind and steady rain didn't seem much of a problem, though I knew a bigger effort would be required later. My elevation that past evening in Wisdom was over 6,000 feet, so the gradual climb was continuing. Long plateaus were now the norm and a significant climb was not far away that would take me over 7,000 feet for the first time.

The Co-Op Girls and I all rode into Jackson, population 26. They were getting ice for their coolers in the van and I stopped for breakfast at the same place. Jackson was a strange little town, with lots of abandoned buildings and virtually no cellphone coverage. As we stopped to eat, I didn't expect much. The pancakes turned out to be really tasty, a fact that the waitress attributed to a special ingredient. I didn't ask and just enjoyed them. The next day, I learned that Jackson area would be the host for most of the summer to a gathering of at least 10,000 people called the Rainbow Gathering, a celebration of peace, love and non-violence. I wondered where these people would get their supplies.

Back out in the rain and headed uphill, the Co-Op Girls passed me two by two. The van stopped again to see if any of us needed anything and soon the Big Hole Pass came into view. I made it close to the top, but walked the last steep mile. A Montana Highway Patrol officer pulled over to ask about my trip, and said he wanted to do something similar. We talked for at least five minutes and he wished me a safe journey. In Montana, few cars go by and just a few minutes later, I was wishing this wasn't the case.

Often, it took just a little preparation for a long downhill. If it was cold or raining, I had to bundle up a little bit. The pace could cause a wind-chill effect that would last for the duration of the downhill. This time, just as I crested the hill, the sun began to shine for the first time all day. I flew downhill on what I thought was a really rough road and soon found out that my rear tire was slowly going flat. I pulled over at the bottom of the hill and pumped it up a little. Once again, I was hoping that the air would hold. This time, it didn't work and I was forced to repair the tire in the deserted Montana high country.

As I mentioned earlier, I had never fixed a tire on my bike. I had watched a video once on how to take the rear tire off, loosening it from the chain and brakes, and dropping it out of the frame. I saw the proper procedure on how to extricate the tube, replace it with another one and complete the rest of the process. But actually doing it all alone was a test of my confidence and ability. As a part-time farmer, all of this stuff made sense to me. I knew the processes on a piece of farm equipment, but now I had no choice but to apply my knowledge to fixing the tire by myself. First up, once again, was to dig my tools and a tube out of the panniers. As my hands got greasy, I tried to keep the grease off the clothes that came out of the bags and were laid on the ground. I got the tire off the rim, pulled out the old tube and checked for anything sticking through the tire. I found nothing, so back in place went the tube liners and the new tube. I pumped the tube up and replaced the wheel, the chain and brakes. Everything looked OK, so I reloaded the bags with all my tools and gear. I rode a little ways and everything seemed fine. I was mildly proud as I said my prayers of thanks.

I thought of the Co-Op Girls, and knew that they were going to take an early afternoon off at the next state park. It was just ahead before the last major climb of the day. I began to realize that I had probably already seen them for the last time and that if all went well, they wouldn't catch me again. There is a short phrase that the long-distance cyclists say to each other when they part company for the expected last time. We just simply say, "Safe travels!" It is a phrase born of the camaraderie of the understood feelings that only the endless hours and shared experiences on a bicycle seat can inspire. I hope they all made it safely to Boston.

On I went to the top of that last climb, Badger Pass. The sun shone brightly now and I was fighting a strong headwind as I climbed this tough mountain. It was the gateway to Dillon, my last stop of the day. Once again, I think I looked pretty bad as two more motorists stopped to offer me water. One offered a ride. "No, I have already over 1,000 miles invested. I have to make every pedal stroke across the country," was my reply. "I can do this!" The driver smiled, we both waved and he drove away.

As I crossed the summit of Badger Pass, once again the wind changed. The wind became a very strong tailwind. The thoughts of my troubling tubes came to mind as I coasted down the hill. Surely Dillon, population 4,382, would have some cellphone service. It was nearly 5 p.m., and I was yet to be off the mountain. I wanted to call the bike shop and see if they could wait for me. I pulled the bike over and called Alternative Bike and Board and Joe answered. Joe was in the first stages of becoming one of my heroes. The wind was howling, the connection was spotty, yet we exchanged enough words that I understood to call when I got into town. On down the hill I went, crossed under Interstate 15 and took Old Highway 91 into town. I called Joe again just as soon as I got inside the city limits, hoping not to miss him. Once again, Joe answered quickly. He listened patiently to my issues with the tubes, asked what bike I rode, and gave me directions to his shop. Joe said, "You make that last turn and then follow the street until you see the house with lots of bikes around it and a fence made out of skis." I told him that I would be there shortly.

I rode down the street and immediately saw the house. The bike shop was in a side yard and I pulled right up to the door. Joe smiled big and started asking about the problems, just as I started taking my gear off the bike. Joe checked both tubes, and replaced the one in the front even though he couldn't find a hole. He oiled the chain and checked out everything else, pronouncing the bike in good shape. I got two spare tubes, and took the slow leaker back for a last chance spare. We loaded the bike up while Joe gave me directions to a motel and Subway. When I asked Joe, "How much do I owe you?", he quickly responded, "Is $10 all right?" I did some quick math and realized that the tubes were worth more than that. I gave him $20, and he didn't want to keep it all. We shook hands, and Joe wished me, "Safe Travels!" Once more, I rode away smiling, confident that my tubes were ready for a lot of miles and that the bike was in good shape. Best of all, I had just met another example of the good people that are all over America. Thank you again, Joe!

My motel on that night was the Motel 6 in Dillon. I asked the clerk if she had an available downstairs room, and she said that she could swap some folks around. Then I asked the price, and got one that is a good bit more than normal for Motel 6, almost $70. The clerk explained that there was nothing else that cheap in town and even called a couple of other places. I had only 71 miles that day, but that total included two mountains and a flat tire repair. I took the room. I soon learned a lesson.

My ride to the Subway was out to a regular highway, in fact the one that I would ride away from town the next morning. The first big sign I spotted was connected to a motel with all rooms for $48 that included a free breakfast. I had learned a big lesson. I considered stopping in to tell the clerk at the Motel 6 desk that she might have deliberately left that one out. The Motel 6 never did fill up overnight, though people on the way to the Rainbow Gathering sat in the yard and a local park. I let the issue go and resolved to do a better job of research next time.

CHAPTER 9
— Dillon, Montana
to Hebgen Lake, Montana —

*Time for some interesting local
gold rush history*

I headed out of town the next morning, reminded once more of the lower price motel and looking forward to a long downhill ride on Highway 41. My route passed Twin Bridges, where I got a good breakfast and stopped at the library to check messages. Cellphone coverage was unavailable again, and this suited me fine most of the time. I had a nice discussion with a local cyclist who told me to beware of some of the roads ahead. Lots of cyclists had gone down in accidents over the years. Next was Sheridan, a happy little town with lots of smiling people. Sheridan also had an Ace Hardware store in the basement of a nice grocery store. I needed some duct tape and picked some up, then got some food and ice cream for the rest of the day. Who knew that you couldn't pay for both at the same cash register? I had to take the duct tape back downstairs and pay separately while they held my groceries upstairs. This was an enjoyable day to sit on the street and eat my ice cream while watching the tractors and cars drive through town. I listened to a political debate between two locals who were intent on presenting their points on the sidewalk.

After my short rest stop, I continued on out of town to yet another downhill. Too many downhills mean a big climb is coming, and this was certainly the case. Today's ride was one of the most interesting to date. I saw the towns coming up and knew that more of the same was on the menu. I was smiling quite a bit myself today. The morning had warmed quite a bit, and the little village of Adler came into view. A water bottle fill-up and two huckleberry ice cream sandwiches took care of any heat issues, and I discussed the area with the clerk. She said that the town had 10,000 residents during the gold rush, but now had about 100. To make matters worse, the store clerk was leaving to live near Greensboro, North Carolina, by the end of the year. Placer mining had ruined the soil for future use, and resulting piles of small rocks were mounded up everywhere.

I waved goodbye and headed out of town toward two towns that I was excited about. Nevada City and Virginia City, Montana, were both famous gold boom towns. Both had made an effort to embrace their history, and it was a pleasure to stop and look through Nevada City. Lots of restored buildings from other parts of Montana had been moved to Nevada City and were now on public display.

My goal was Virginia City, where I hoped to spend the night. I had been climbing steadily as I rode into the western end of the beautifully restored town. My first stop was into the visitor's center for directions and advice. I was told that most of the shops and restaurants would all start to close about 6 p.m., but that the saloon had a pretty good grill and it would remain open later. There was no grocery store in town. I asked about a campground and was glad to hear that one was available. My last question was probably the most important and a good insight into the way people perceive things. I said simply, "How far to the top of the mountain?" The lady said, "About 3 miles." The man said, "More like 5 or 6." They proceeded to discuss the distance and arrived at a consensus of 4.5 miles.

I left and headed up the hill with the intent of stopping at a campground just past the city limits. I finally found it and was told that cyclists could camp for free. I set up my tent and decided to walk back down to the town to find some food. I did take time to ask the owner, "How far to the top of the hill?" His replied, "About 9 miles." Choices of food were not abundant and I ended up with two grilled cheese sandwiches, not nearly enough. More fun was walking around town and looking at all the old buildings and the historical plaques on them. I did that for quite a while, then got ice cream before heading back to the campground.

As I walked to the campground, a woman in a truck stopped to ask me where I was going. I didn't know exactly how to respond, since the right answer could be the campground or North Carolina, or possibly even South Carolina. I replied, "I have my bike up here at the campground." She just quietly drove away. I guess it wasn't the right answer. I headed on to bed without a shower because there was not an open one. I wondered who was right about the distance to the top of the mountain. Regardless, this had been a good day.

The next day dawned clear and cool as I arose early, but all I could think about was the dog that barked all night in the campground. All night! I packed up quickly, and headed out to see just how far the top of the hill actually was from the campground. The climb turned out to be steep, but only a little over three miles. Best surprise I had all day. I had to walk the top of it. Another nice surprise came as I met three cross-country cyclists, all headed down into Virginia City. The spokesperson of the group said that the three hadn't known each other before they started riding, and now they traveled together every day. They were all happy and positive and we exchanged information. They reminded me that there were lots of breakfast spots in Ennis, the next town. I told them there is little food in Virginia City, but wished them "Safe Travels!" and hopes for a good breakfast.

I coasted quickly into Ennis, Montana, and saw three other cyclists on the way up the mountain. After exchanging information with the last one, we headed our separate ways. I dreaded the climb for him, but knew that it wouldn't be long before I would have another one, too. Upon entering Ennis, I made a mistake. I was more than hungry and didn't take time to ask about the best possible breakfast restaurant. There were several choices, and I stopped at the second place. I saw the menu and wished that I hadn't. Pancakes are always on my mind in the mornings, and here was a day when I really needed them after going to bed hungry the night before. I was disappointed to learn that one pancake was small and would cost $3.25. Two were $6. My tactic quickly changed to "get the best deal you can." I smiled at the waitress and told her that I wanted one pancake and asked, "Could you get the cook to make it big?" I added two eggs. I hadn't had a shower or a shave in a couple of days, and my cycling clothes needed washing. Maybe she just agreed to get me out of there, but I did get a much bigger pancake than their normal. I also looked around and noticed that only one other table was being used, while the traffic seemed to be going into a café right down the street. Another lesson learned.

On to a much tougher day of climbing than I expected. My maps didn't show it, but I stopped at a fly fishing shop and got the real scoop. Lots of climbing and few choices for a motel were just ahead. Between Ennis and West Yellowstone, there were again lots of secluded areas. My plan was to get the best deal I could on a room and get cleaned up, right after the endless climbing.

I passed over two dams and rolled past a small ranger station just as I came up one of the most unusual areas of my whole trip. A small lake, now known as Quake Lake, had been the home of a busy campground back in the late 1950s. One night, with almost a full campground, a natural disaster killed nearly all of the guests as an earthquake and the resulting flood created a new and much bigger lake. It was eerie in this area as many of the tops of the flooded trees still protruded above the water.

I stopped at the Kirkwood Resort, on Hebgen Lake's Marina, but still about 20 miles from West Yellowstone. Chances remained strong that I would be camping for two nights in the Yellowstone area. I asked for the best deal Kirkwood had on a room, and was rewarded with the Grizzly Cabin for an embarrassing amount of money, about twice what I usually paid. Prices in the resort store were high and ice for the cabin was not free. The clerk had plenty of surprises including the following statement, "Well, we only have the one cabin left. You can take it or leave it. We'll eventually get someone who can't find a room in Yellowstone who wants it." I took it, hurting the whole time. What I did get was a spectacular view of a beautiful lake, and a nicely furnished cabin that would have been great for a weeklong stay.

My Surly bike continued to perform perfectly. It remained dependable and had taken some abuse with rough roads and early consistent rain. The all-important seat had formed to my own rear well and I had no thoughts of a saddle sore. I was tired of carrying my backpack and noticed that other cyclists have a small case mounted on their handlebars for "need to be close" things such as wallet, phone, etc. The backpack had started to come apart. I decided to ditch the backpack for handlebar bag. My panniers kept my other gear totally dry.

Speaking of gear, I desperately needed a better tent. I had broken one of my fiberglass poles and the tent leaked. It was not big enough for me to sit up in, and I needed more room to get dressed inside. My plan was to stop in West Yellowstone to check out a new one, just before several possible nights in the National Park campgrounds. My other gear continued doing exactly what was expected of it. Additional CO_2 cartridges for pumping bike tires were on my list, but not critical.

My body had only a few small issues. My head had been sunburned and so had my ears. I began wearing a cap in the brightest sun. Muscle-wise, my arms and shoulders had been regularly tired and sometimes sore. Leg muscles, especially the quadriceps, had been pushed harder than ever and have held up. My toes went numb daily, but just a few minutes off the bike got the blood flowing again.

My thoughts drifted toward the next morning. I would get to Yellowstone early, and chances were good that I would meet up with some great friends from home. Wyoming was just a few hours away. From the start, I knew Yellowstone would be an expected highlight. I would see it tomorrow.

CHAPTER 10
— West Yellowstone, Montana to Yellowstone National Park, Wyoming —

Meeting some friends from home for a picnic

Every morning, I asked God to ride with me through the day. Then, near the end of the day, I recapped with Him what had happened, and again asked for His guidance. Although occasional weather issues made for trying times, so far, there had been no real danger or reason to worry. Wide lanes or occasional separate bike lanes made much of the riding easy. With no worry about traffic, a cyclist can concentrate on other issues such as holes in the road, low-hanging limbs and watching for road signs. Traffic and a few other issues were about to become much more of a problem, putting extra stress on this cyclist.

My ride into West Yellowstone was an easy one, with the 20 miles passing quickly. I was excited to get close to the best-known national park in the United States. Just the thought of riding through it on a bike seemed full of magic, as I was reminded again of my ride in West Virginia. My friends from home, Meredith and Andy Abramson, were going to visit the park on that same day, and we had a tentative plan to meet later. Lesser things, like seeing Old Faithful, were going to be fun, too.

This was an exciting morning for me, but I was also on a mission. I had to find a usable and dependable tent. The one that I had used so far was not at all what it was represented to be. The weight of the tent made it one of the lighter choices on the market. It was a one-person tent, just what I wanted. It was easy to get in and out of. It had been reasonably priced. That ended the list of superlatives. I quickly realized once my journey started that the tent was going to be crucial. Most days, it would quietly ride along bungeed to the back of the bike. My goal for every day, if possible, was to find a reasonably priced motel room. That goal was unrealistic because of the space between significant towns. In the beginning, I did not know much about hostels and was wary of them. The tent would be used on days that I couldn't be inside at night. The first few weeks, my attempts at sleeping in a tent had not gone well. I was extremely sore the next morning, at least in some parts of my body. After one night in a campground, I woke up with a hip pointer that took a couple of days to go away. I also needed just a little more room, and hoped to be able to sit up in the new tent and also have some room to put a few pieces of gear inside if rain threatened. The new tent had to be watertight, without a doubt. Rains had been only light and moderate so far, yet the tent had leaked each time I used it. Finally and perhaps most importantly, I needed to be able to quickly set up and break down the new tent. So, was it possible to find a reasonably priced tent in one of the priciest vacation areas in America? To make matters worse, I entered the Yellowstone area on the first Saturday of Independence week, the busiest week of the season.

I also had to load up on groceries. I had been warned by several cyclists and at least one store owner that the Yellowstone area would be the priciest of the whole journey. Once inside the park, prices would be even worse. I planned to have a full stomach as I rode into the park, and that would happen just on the east side of West Yellowstone.

As soon as I rolled into town, I stopped at another fly fishing store and asked for the best place to find a quality, yet reasonably priced tent. They recommended a store just another block down the street, and shortly before 9 a.m., I went in search of my perfect tent. The clerk listened intently, nodding often while I asked for the things I wanted. He took me back to the tent area and immediately pulled out a fairly light and small tent bag. So far, so good. He told me that I could set this tent up in 3-5 minutes tops and the same for breaking it down. Next, he said that versions of this same tent were used on Mt. Everest. I was almost hooked when the clerk said, "I have this very same model, and I don't plan on buying another tent." I asked the big question, "So how much is it?" I dreaded the answer, but knew I needed something much better than I had. The clerk replied that the tent was on sale for just over $400. I quickly told him that I couldn't pay that much. Truthfully, I could have, but sure didn't want to. I asked again, and probably pleaded a little, "If you will make me a really good deal, and then show me how to set it up, I'll buy the tent but I can't pay $400." The clerk told me that there would be no cheap tents in this town because there is such a demand. I stood there just a couple of minutes and said, "Just give me the best deal you can." He sold me the tent for less than $300, then showed me how to set it up and repack it. I count the clerk as another hero because I learned a lot about tents and left with one that made me comfortable when camping for the rest of the trip.

Next stop was for groceries. I asked the tent clerk for the best place in town, and he smiled and sent me where he shops. It was just another block away in this Disney World kind of town, and I parked the bike, promptly put my original tent in the trash can, and strapped the new one to the bike. Now I was focused on groceries. The selections were pretty good, but I was shocked by the prices. Cookies, pastries and bananas were nearly double what I had bought them for in the Safeway store just a few days earlier. None of the customers were looking at the prices. They were running through and grabbing things, hoping to get into Yellowstone as quickly as possible. Just as the store management knew, I had no choice but to suffer the over-inflated prices. I started to get an uneasy feeling about this Yellowstone area.

I called the town of West Yellowstone a Disney World kind of town. A good bit of it reminded me of the area around Orlando. Lots of bear and wolf displays replaced the alligator exhibits of Florida, and people seemed willing to pay any exorbitant price because they were on vacation. Drivers were neither as careful nor courteous as I had seen before, especially those who hurried to get ahead just one more place in the line to Yellowstone's entrance. This was a sign of things to come.

Everyone pays to enter Yellowstone, even hikers and cyclists. I sat in a slow-moving line, breathing exhaust fumes for about 10 minutes, then pulled boldly to the front of the line. I leaned my bike against a column, quickly paid the fee, grabbed the receipt and was on my way. About six lanes merged together as we headed into the park. The first sign was one that listed all the campgrounds in the park, and I noticed that seven of them were already noted as full. I found out more about that later.

My first few miles in the park were congested, but with a narrow shoulder. The traffic kept stopping and starting. Just a few miles into the park, I crossed into Wyoming. It was the saddest looking state sign that I would see. Ten miles into the park, traffic stopped quickly for no apparent reason. I kept on pedaling, until a lady quickly opened her door and sat there with the door open. I couldn't get by, so I slid off into the gravel beside her dual axle truck. She noticed me and said, "Oh, are you OK?" But she didn't close the door. There would be more of the same. Vehicles would usually stop if they spotted an animal of some kind, which was fine with me. But I hoped they would stay in the lane as they did it. Yellowstone roads were built many years ago and are narrow. Most of the time, there were no shoulders and often there was brush growing right up the edge of the asphalt. Modern wide campers, especially the buses, were as wide as the lanes. There was almost no room for the cyclists. I wondered how many times a cyclist had been clipped in the park. I didn't want to find out first-hand.

Offsetting the road hazards was a scenic ride, especially early on as I pedaled alongside the Madison River. Old Faithful was my focal point, and I hoped to get there just about the same time as the Abramsons from Salisbury did. Meredith had planned a picnic, and it was going to be a treat to see them. Old Faithful is about 30 miles into the park, and most of the ride is a steady climb. It was fun to ride along and see other geysers along the way. Signs for trailheads were along the road, and occasionally I passed the entrance to a campground. But mostly I kept pedaling, with an eye on my mirror watching for tight traffic situations developing behind me. Traffic heading west, at least in the morning, was not heavy. This gave those drivers who were going around me a little more room and I was thankful for that.

The climb was getting tougher as I got close to Old Faithful. In mid afternoon, I heard a rather noisy group approaching from the rear and realized that the Abramson family had arrived. I pulled over about five miles from the Old Faithful area and we all hugged and visited briefly, still amazed that we had found each other so easily on the other side of America. We headed on to the famous geyser area, with the Abramsons planning on setting up their picnic. The first real rain of the day broke out about this time, and it soon became a downpour complete with some hail. I pedaled on while they tried to find the picnic area. It seemed that the parking lot outside Old Faithful is more than two miles off the main road. By this time, I was hungry and ready to get off the bike for a while.

Seeing the main geyser had been a goal since I first thought of the ride and which route to take. All the traffic seemed to be heading the same way as I was, and I soon found two huge parking lots. There had to be room for easily more than a thousand cars. Just like Disney World, I thought. Once again, I was wary of what might happen. The Abramsons found me as I rolled into the parking lot and we enjoyed a fantastic meal of real food, probably the best and healthiest of my trip so far. We knew the scheduled time for the next eruption and headed toward a huge line of bleachers surrounded by several large rustic buildings. We milled around the area, waiting. Once again and right on time, as it has for hundreds of years, Old Faithful sent steam aloft. Some in the crowd cheered and others oohed and aahed. We made lots of great pictures and then it was over. The Abramsons got ready to leave, and after lots of goodbyes they headed on to their next stop. Now things would get interesting.

My mileage total for the day was at almost 50. It was about 4:30 p.m. Skies were cloudy and it looked like darkness would fall early. I wanted to ask a park ranger what my options were on finding a campground, so I walked to an information desk and asked just that question. I was told once again that none of the campgrounds were close and that I would need to call the reservation number anyway. She promptly handed me a publication that had this number and I was dismissed. While sitting outside, I dialed the number and went through an endless recording. Reservations for campgrounds for the rest of 2013 and 2014 were being taken and there were lots of directions to go through. I just wanted to ask about an available campground.

Finally, a pleasant sounding young man came on the phone and asked me what he could do to help. I immediately asked for an available campground near Old Faithful and hopefully headed east from where I was because I was pedaling across country. I described myself as a single cyclist. I ended with, "It is going to get dark and probably rain some more, and I would like to be getting set for the night." His response knocked me backwards when he said, "So sir, what size is your RV?" I thought then that he wasn't paying attention and got a little more frustrated than I should have. My next response was, "I said I am a cyclist headed east. I don't have an RV." His response, "So, what size is your tent?" I answered quickly, "About four by six feet." He then told me that seven of the 10 campgrounds were full and one more would close at 7 p.m., but it was 20 miles away to the west. I said again, "I am headed east and want to go that way."

As the conversation became more ridiculous, he said, "But sir, you can do what we call back country camping. There are designated areas about four miles off the main road where you can camp legally. You have to hike in." My immediate response, "What would I do with my bike? Plus, I don't have time for something like that. So what is wrong with me just finding an open spot in the park and setting up my tent?" He replied, "Well, sir, I am at work, and I have to inform you that you would then face a fine of $250. I do have two rooms at the hotel there at Old Faithful that are each available for $250. Want me to check on that?"

This conversation was clearly taking a lot of time and I had made no progress. I said to the young man, "What campgrounds are open, and when do they close? And what happens if I get to one after it closes?" Confusing me even more, he said, "There are three campgrounds open, but none of them are headed east out of the park. Plus, to hold a site, you will have to reserve it with me." I replied, "What if I reserve one and don't get there in time?" His response, "Well, you should try to get there." He gave me the three campgrounds and I checked my maps, then thanked him for his time. One of them, Grant Village, was in fact on my way. It was now past 5 p.m., and I had two of the biggest Yellowstone mountains and over 25 miles to go. The situation didn't look good.

I left the Old Faithful area confused but determined. I had less than four hours to make the Grant Village campground and virtually no idea what to expect. After struggling to get back on the main road, I headed north. Traffic at that time of day was thankfully less, but the common pattern was a minute or so of nobody passing, then a slow moving camper would lead a long line of vehicles by me in a short period of time. The rain came sporadically, but was never heavy. Craig Pass and a continental divide were both well over 8,000 feet in elevation and steep. Lots of trees made the views unspectacular and the climbing seem endless. Finally, after three hours, I topped this continental divide and had a nice downhill toward Grant Village and what I might find there. I came upon several vehicles parked beside the road and a frenzy of people running back and forth. I asked what was happening and was informed that there was a bull moose just on the other side of trees. I quickly stopped and also quickly fell off the bike as I hurried too fast to see it. No damage this time except to my ego because it happened right in front of this frenzied crowd. The moose was incredibly large and was just easily grazing as he ambled along. Some people ran up and stood right beside him as they took photos. At about that time, park rangers began to arrive and disperse the crowd. The moose could become violent quickly, they warned. I headed for the campground.

One note about the continental divides should be explained. There were multiple crossings of the continental divide in the park and at other times on the journey. The continental divide signifies the point where any water on the west side would flow west and on the east would flow east. They were always at the top of a mountain and also after significant climbs. There is a whole bicycle trail called the Continental Divide Trail, which has not been that appealing to me.

The sun had set as I neared the Grant Village campground, which turned out to be a huge village more than a mile off the road. I pushed on even though all the signs said "Campground Full." I passed a gas station and a large restaurant. There was a post office and an RV dumping station. Lots of traffic was going both ways. I found the campground office and stopped hopefully to put an end to my dilemma of where to spend the night. The time was now nearing 9 p.m., but a steady line of people were still checking in with reservations. I asked, "Do you have a campsite available?" Her quick response came with a smile, "Yes, we always have campsites for cyclists and hikers! All the large campgrounds do." She quickly signed me up for an outlying site for a nominal price of less than $7. I got a warning about making sure that I put any food in the bear box. She said, "You must do that. You are in their territory now."

I quickly set up my brand-new tent and it performed just as advertised. I wondered about a bear box and where I could find one.

My food at that time included bananas, power bars and Pop-Tarts. My campsite was absolutely on the edge of the big complex and adjoined huge, dense woods. After not locating a bear box quickly, I took a chance and kept my food close by. Regardless, I headed for bed with a strange contentment of having made some headway in the confusing system of Yellowstone campgrounds. I later heard of similar problems from other cyclists.

It was a short night, with daylight coming soon after 5 a.m. The bears hadn't disturbed my campsite, so I jumped up to pack up and get ready to leave the area on my way east. I thought briefly about how interesting it would be to once again talk with the young man on the reservation line and tell him how things had worked out well for me. Instead, I headed to the huge restaurant for a much needed breakfast. I did find cellphone coverage there and was able to submit my travel updates back to the newspaper. After an overpriced breakfast buffet, I was glad to head out for a long day that would include my exit of Yellowstone and entrance into the Grand Teton National Park, both of which included huge challenges.

First up was my ride to cover some rolling terrain that set my way out of the park as I headed east. This area did have some beautiful scenery including some amazing rivers. It also had endless traffic heading the same way I was. Many of the drivers were impatient as they waited to get around me while I pedaled uphill. A few didn't like the delay and expressed themselves as they passed by. Most were polite and it was always pleasant for me to see the friendly waves of those who appreciated my effort. Still the scariest thing I saw was an occasional RV passing just inches from my handlebars.

I pedaled on to the exit of Yellowstone and stopped to ask directions of one of the rangers. She told me that I would love the Grand Tetons and that the roads were better with more room. There would be less traffic and the scenery from the roads would be better. She also said, "I would never ride a bike in Yellowstone." I totally understood and was frankly glad to be exiting the over-trafficked area.

Later, I found a statistic that said more than 90 percent of tourists never left the main roads of Yellowstone for the most spectacular scenery.

Official rear wheel dipping at Seaside Beach, Oregon, on the Pacific Ocean.

One of the many Pacific Ocean overlooks along the Oregon coast.

Snake River, Oregon. Site of my first flat tire.

Spectacular scenery in western Oregon.

A lot of roads on the journey were friendly to cyclists, such as this one in Oregon.

Open grazing in ranching country of Idaho. This bull is all alone.

Little Salmon River, Idaho. Wide shoulders and downhill for miles.

Severe weather in Montana. I kept riding.

Near Togwotee Pass, Wyoming. Battling flies and mosquitoes at the peak.

Rock formations in the Wind River Canyon.

My bike was shipped to Astoria, Oregon and reassembled at Bikes and Beyond.

I was headed to Rosedale, when Benny Martin stopped to help me with a flat tire. He later found me in a church hostel that night to bring me more CO_2 cartridges.

Above: I met the Abramson family, also from my hometown of Salisbury, N.C, in Yellowstone National Park. Old Faithful is in the background.
Right: Matthias Erb, from Berlin, Germany, got a 90-day visa to bike across the United States.

The Grand Tetons, the most spectacular mountain range on the whole trip.

The 100-plus year-old Hotel Eastin, in Kremmling, Colorado, my favorite hotel. Zane Grey wrote a novel here.

Highest point of my ride, the Hoosier Pass in Colorado at 11,539 feet.

The worst night of my adventure was spent here, including chipping a tooth.
Never spend a night over a bar if you need to sleep.

I was glad to get to Kansas, leaving the biting flies and Dust Bowl area of Colorado behind.

Grain elevators were the landmarks in Kansas. I could see them from 10 miles away due to the flat land.

The Ozark hills in Missouri made for some tough climbing.

Best ice cream of the trip at Spooner's in Ellington, Missouri. I had two pine-apple milkshakes, just 30 minutes apart.

Crossing the Mississippi River at Chester, Illinois.

Ready to cross the Ohio River at Cave-In-Rock, Illinois.

The most interesting character of the trip was "Mountain Man." He charged me a dollar to see this preserved creature and told me that he was going to be lowered into the Ohio River, locked in a casket.

People could keep up with my trip through my daily column in the Salisbury Post.

I loved this sign. With more than one meaning, it reminded me how each pedal stroke was taking me closer home. Now more than halfway.

A replica of Abraham Lincoln's boyhood home at Knob Creek, Kentucky.

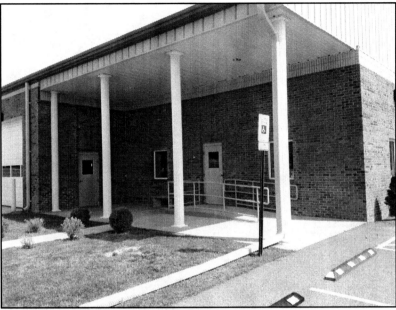

The new fire house in Utica, Kentucky. It is open to cyclists daily. I saw the best lightning show ever while here.

Gary fixed the grinding of the lower gears on my bicycle in Damascus, Virginia. He wouldn't take any money for doing it.

It was late on a long day when I saw this welcome sign. The home stretch.

My last night camping, just inside North Carolina. I spent the night behind Maria Hurtado's convenience store.

SecondFront

news@salisburypost.com

INTO THE ATLANTIC

Coast-to-coast bike journey ends beside shore at Myrtle Beach

Editor's note: David Freeze has just finished cycling coast to coast. His trek started June 10 in Oregon. His dispatches from the road have been published in the newspaper, at www.salisburypost.com, and on his blog, "Gotta Run" at blog.salisburypost.com/gottarun

Sunday, Aug. 4

David Freeze

My day started like so many of the previous 54 days did. Up early, repacking the stuff in my bike bags and excited about the possibilities that the day could hold. I left Bennettsville after grabbing a light breakfast and wanting to make plenty of headway before the beach traffic started to build. Most of the terrain was flat, and I was pushing the pace. Highway 38 didn't have much traffic, but it sure had rough roads. Regardless, 25 miles flew by. Then, I met the heavy traffic on Highway 501 as I turned directly toward the beach.

I was greeted by my nemesis from Kentucky, the dreaded rumble strips. Once again, nowhere to ride but on the roads. The same courteous driving continued from the day before, and people gave me plenty of room. We got through Aynor and then Conway. On occasion there were shoulders. The closer to Myrtle Beach I got, the safer I felt. The stop lights slowed down the traffic, and less speed and occasional shoulders got me to the beach safely.

My first ice cream came just after 80 miles, and by that time, it was much needed. My gas tank was on empty. I found the motel at just after 88 miles.

Norma and Mark Honeycutt, along with Bradley Eagle, came down to see and film the front-wheel dipping. Norma made the

David Freeze dipped the rear wheel of his bicycle into the Pacific Ocean in Oregon at the beginning of his trip June 10. On Sunday, he dipped the front wheel into the Atlantic Ocean at Myrtle Beach to complete his long journey.

Astoria, Ore.

— 4,164 total miles —

Myrtle Beach, S.C.

I just told Bradley that now my life will return to its regular world. There was a feeling of contentment each evening after a successful day of riding, and the subsequent planning for the next day. I will certainly miss the adventure and uncertainty of each day. There will always remain a great sense of awe for me, even

certainly nice for me having so many of you check in as I made the trip. As the events of the last few days have shown, I had lots of support and interest from Oregon to South Carolina, across this great country for a total of 4,164

The Salisbury Post ran a big story on the wheel dipping in the Atlantic Ocean at Myrtle Beach.

CHAPTER 11
— Grand Tetons National Park, Wyoming to Rawlins, Wyoming —

A brief harsh encounter, then more enjoyable riding on the other side of Yellowstone

This day was warming quickly and I pedaled up a long hill and headed toward the Grand Tetons. Quickly, I spotted the largest and most amazing mountains on my right as I rode on much better roads. My goal was to cover over 40 miles to reach Coulter Bay, a large campground complex with food and plenty of water. I began to see lots of signs about road work ahead and "Yield to Cyclists." What I found was Sunday and Independence week paving in the park, causing 30-minute delays. As we entered the area, I saw new paving and stayed in line as we approached the stopping point. Drivers were upset with the delay but had no choice except to wait for a pilot truck to lead them to the other end of a one-mile work area.

At that point, the stuff hit the fan. I pulled up to follow the other traffic around me as we would head through the road work. I was told, "You can't ride through here. You will have to load your bike on the pilot truck and ride on that truck to the other end." I disagreed and told them that I would bicycle through this area, one way or another. A supervisor was called to deal with me, and I informed him that I was riding across the country and was not going to void it because of some silly rule. He then called his supervisor, who eventually arrived after a long delay. I was almost out of water and it was now hot, especially in the area of the new pavement. The latest supervisor told me that I could just add this one mile to the end of my ride. I angrily explained that the end of my ride would be at the Atlantic Ocean, and I could not ride a mile out into the ocean. She said, "Sir, we cannot allow you to ride through this area." I quickly responded, "Then you will have to physically stop me. I will ride through here, and I will do it very soon. I am out of water and need to get some soon." One of their group quickly told me that I could be physically stopped, to which I replied, "I don't think you can." For some reason, the stalemate was broken as the latest supervisor walked over and told me that I could follow her to the other end. She asked me to stay close. My anger subsided as I pushed the pace and quickly passed through the paving area. I pulled into the convenience store and the supervisor pulled over ahead of me. I wondered what I would face as I came back out. The total delay was nearly an hour.

I filled up on water and got some ice cream, then found a spot under the shade to plan the rest of my day. Once I had a plan, I pulled back into the paving area. I waved to the supervisor as I took a right and pedaled on without any issues. My frustration soon dissolved, but I was ready to be out of these national parks. As I reached Moran Junction, I took a left onto Highway 26/287, a much less traveled road. Most of the vehicles went in other directions and suddenly I was rewarded with a wonderful quiet. The sound of endless vehicles passing had ceased. I wondered if I had made a mistake, but resolved that with another look at my maps. I relaxed more than I had in two days.

Now, I needed to find a place to spend the night and two possibilities were on the road soon. One was a campground, but it was hot and the bugs were flying, so I rode on to the next one. It was the only motel for miles, and the rates were expensive. My map listed a hostel onsite, and I asked about that. She offered a private room with a shared bathroom for over $90 or an Indian teepee with a bunk for $20. I thought of the heat and bugs and took the room, and bargained the price down to less than $70. It was Sunday night and the Yankees were playing, and I hoped to catch some of it. That would be worth something in the still over-priced room. In a unique twist, the TV didn't work in my room and she gave me another room just to use the TV. Two rooms for the price of one made the deal a little better.

I slept well and headed on out the next morning for the largest climb of the trip yet. Togwotee Pass was at 9,658 feet. It was a much cooler morning and I wanted to get a good start on the climb. There were also two other cyclists staying in the same hostel, and I hoped to be ahead of them. I never met them, even though we shared a bathroom. I did find out they were husband and wife, traveling on a tandem bike. The climbing again went on and on until I finally crossed the pass after battling mosquitoes and flies on the windless morning. Total road distance was 18.5 miles to make the summit.

My next destination was Dubois, Wyoming, known as the jack-alope capital of the world. Dubois was a town of less than 1,000 people but it seemed to have everything. Plenty of tourist stops and at least six motels. I found a grocery store and loaded up a nearly depleted pannier with food. This would have been a perfect place for a rest day, but the weather was too good. I saw brief signs that the upcoming scenery might be special.

I parked my bike outside the store, and took a chance to see if there was an available WiFi. There was, and I checked my messages and laid my iPad across the top of my tent that was strapped to the bike. I grabbed my wallet and went in the store and leisurely looked for some good food, made my selections, and checked out. I had totally forgotten about my iPad! Just as I had left it, it remained on the top of my tent and untouched. There was a constant flow of people passing the bike, any of whom could easily have taken it. But in another display of faith, and goodness of America, nobody did.

The Wind River Canyon and Indian Reservation soon captured all of my attention. For miles in all directions, the canyon had colors that seemed painted and unending. As the clouds and sun passed over, the colors seemed to change before my eyes. I was mesmer-ized! This was the most amazing area, and the best scenery that I would see on the whole journey across America. The biggest surprise was that little traffic was here. It didn't matter to me as I had almost a full bike lane, but after the rush-rush to see the scenery of Yellowstone, it was the perfect environment to enjoy a long look around at my own pace. This afternoon was a top highlight of the whole trip. Gradually, and with a few hills, I pulled away from the area. Never did I see anybody trying to sell services or goods for highly inflated prices. The reservation is the home of the Shoshoni and Arapahoe tribes. The Wind River Canyon, encompassing almost 2 million acres, totally surpassed the more famous national parks for me. It is the one sight that I hope to see again.

My maps called for the next town being Fort Washakie. It was going to be a long ride, so I pulled over at the crossroads of Crowheart to ask a few questions. Both of these areas are still in the Wind River Reservation. I found the Crowheart Store, which also houses the local post office, and asked about possible camping sites. The proprietor, Laura Arnold, told me that it would be fine to camp under the overhang at the fire department across the road. Storms were in the area, and it was almost 7 p.m. I thought the overhang would be a great place to spend the night and went back across to the store to get some food and ice cream. I got great tips about the upcoming ride, and was informed that the next real town coming up would be Lander. Laura said that Lander was a "real town" because it even had a McDonald's. The night was uneventful, and I had the magical opportunity to watch several storm cells as they passed. Watching such a display of lightning in Wyoming was better than any TV show that I have ever seen.

I rolled out early the next morning, thinking back that people like Laura Arnold were exactly what I hoped to find on my journey. She was genuine and helpful, even though she was dealing with a gas pump power outage while I was there.

Fort Washaskie was next, and I stopped at the post office hoping to pick up a package that had been shipped to me. It wasn't there yet, but I did have an animated talk with the postmaster and one of her clerks. I was told, "Don't you just love Wyoming? You won't have any problems with the locals." Of course, she was right. I rode on out of town after getting the largest cinnamon bun that I had ever seen.

I made tentative plans to spend the night at free camping in Sweetwater Station. But first, I had to pass through Lander. Other cyclists told me that Lander was one of the most bicycle-friendly towns on the whole TransAmerica Trail. The wide bicycle lanes were spectacular and I rolled into town quickly on them. I planned a stop for lunch at Subway or McDonald's where I hoped to use their WiFi. Subway was so crowded that it would take too long to get any food there, so I headed for McDonald's. As I was riding down the road, a nice-looking lady in an SUV pulled up beside me and asked, "Have you enjoyed your trip so far? Where are you headed? I answered both questions, and she replied, "Well, we are glad to have you here in Lander!" I thanked her and smiled again as she pulled away. There was so much good left in America.

A stop for lunch at McDonald's ended up in my meeting two groups of cyclists, one headed east and one west. We all exchanged information, and I knew that I would be challenged to stay ahead of the two guys who were also headed east. They looked young and fit and also had Surly bikes. My WiFi responsibilities taken care of and plenty of oatmeal raisin cookies in my bags, I headed toward the next climb just before Sweetwater Station. The climbing was through more of a high desert, with an occasional ranch. I made it over the pass, and actually enjoyed the climb for the most part. I was getting stronger. The guys behind me hadn't come in sight yet, but I knew they would soon.

After 89 miles, I rolled into a rest area at Sweetwater Station, named for a nearby river. Legend said that a mule loaded with sugar once lost his balance and fell into the river. There were lots of covered picnic areas. I thought briefly that this was where I was supposed to camp but soon found the correct site at a Mormon facility across the road. This crossroad is part of the famous Overland Stage Coach route and near the even more famous Pony Express area. Two other groups of cyclists had joined me at the Mormon Church property. One group was the two riders who I had met in Lander. I did beat them here and felt good about that. A bit of a challenge, probably left over from my running days. Sadly, just before they entered the park, the two guys collided on their cycles and damaged the front tire of one bike. They messed with it later and thought they had it fixed. Lots of first aid helped with their injuries. The Mormons provided water and a restroom, but they also provided a few rules. One included no hair washing, and another said that we couldn't leave any trash in their trash cans. We were glad to comply, but I knew I would be ready to leave early the next morning.

I rose at 5 a.m. at first light and packed up my gear. There was no movement from the tents of the other cyclists. I had slept for the second straight night on top of a table and under a roof that provided good sight of the stars. The stars looked so big to me during the night that I marveled at them. It was also a cold night. Thankfully, my sleeping bag did its job and I remained comfortable. But after packing the bike, I was ready to go when I noticed a cute lady had come to sit on my picnic table. Laurie was Mormon and her family had come to Sweetwater Station from Chicago, hoping to expose her kids to a slice of Mormon history. Sweetwater Station was used as a gathering point for a group who long ago rescued other Mormons trapped in a snowstorm in the mountains. She was fun to talk with, and it appeared that nobody else in the campground was up. After a nice discussion, she sent me on my way with several bags of sliced fruit. Still another good person that I will remember forever and I smiled again as I rode away.

On the road a little later than I hoped at 6:30 a.m., I soon realized that there were few hills in the area. I made 40 miles by 11 a.m., and considered stopping for breakfast. The next town was

Jeffrey City, an unusual town with lots of empty military-style bar-racks across the road. I saw a bar that served breakfast, but decided to keep rolling. I soon spotted Split Rock, an unusual rock forma-tion that was a landmark for the Pony Express, Overland Stage Trail, and many others. Next came Muddy Gap with one store and Lamont with a café. The café didn't look too appealing, plus I had loaded up on food at the store in Muddy Gap. I also met two ladies in their 60s who get together each summer to spend a few weeks knocking out another section of the TransAmerica trail. They were also headed east while riding recumbent bikes. I hoped to see them again, but doubted that I would. They were already planning to call it a day at the first opportunity.

It was in this area that the famous Pony Express route inter-sected the TransAmerica trail. The Pony Express riders covered a 1,966 mile route between St. Joseph, Missouri, and Sacramento, California. Each rider rode about 75 miles, exchanging horses every 10-12 miles. Total time for the mail crossing was about 10 days. The Pony Express was only used from 1860 to 1862.

Shortly afterward, near Lamont, I found the road had deterio-rated and was falling apart. Even with a tailwind, this section was going to be tough. Then it got worse. The asphalt shoulders were a part of new construction and had been ground up for replacement soon. It was soft and small gravel, and I could not ride on it. Once again, I was back in the traffic lanes amid significant traffic. It be-came quite a battle, but the ride had a safe ending. I climbed over two more continental divides, and then with 90 miles complete, ended up in Rawlins, Wyoming.

I got lots of help from locals at the McDonald's on directions and a reasonably priced room. I called one place across the street and was happy with the price. While walking the bike across the highway, I spotted another motel next door. I walked to it, just to make sure I was making the right choice. A lady came down the stairs, sat down at a big desk and quoted me $120 a night, then told me I wouldn't find one any less in this town. I told her I already had, then walked back next door and took the room for half that price.

After 25 days on the road, I had been in four states and was approaching Colorado. My mileage total at this point was 1,667 or about 39 percent of my way across America. Things had gone well, and I was sure that prayers were the key to that success.

CHAPTER 12
— Rawlins, Wyoming to Pueblo, Colorado —

Climbing challenges and high altitude scenery

This chapter will include the longest and highest climb of the whole journey and the biggest descent. Long climbs continued to reward my legs with long periods of coasting.

After traversing a short connecting road, I took the entrance ramp onto the interstate. It was totally cool to be riding my bike on the interstate, something that isn't allowed in most states. The TransAmerica course would use interstates again, but this time it had me riding about 20 miles on the smooth and wide super highway. There was a lot of traffic, but I had a wide lane all to myself. I had learned that the better the road, the less likely it was to have steep climbs. This was certainly the case on this day. It was a bright and sunny morning.

I exited Interstate 80 at Walcott, Wyoming, and headed through a rolling section toward Saratoga. The only scenery was lots of pasture land. Traffic began to increase, with lots of people-loaded vehicles going by. Few vehicles came back from Saratoga toward me, so I thought that something to do with the Fourth of July might be happening in Saratoga. I felt a little homesick for the opportunity to celebrate America's birthday. I planned to stop and join in, especially if there was a parade. As I got closer, I heard an announcer and a band. It was a parade, and a real western-style one at that.

The road through the center of town, and my mapped route, was blocked by the parade. I pulled over to the next block, got some ice cream and a drink, then settled in to watch the rest of the parade. That parade was full of horses and all the dignitaries were either in wagons, carriages or on horseback. A parade in Wyoming was almost as good as being back home for the parade in Faith, North

Carolina. I watched as the parade queen rode by on her horse, surrounded by others girls on their horses, too. All were dressed in their western best. As the parade ended, no one was in a hurry to leave. They stood around in groups and talked and not a single person made a move to clean up the horse manure. That was my kind of parade.

Two other cyclists, both heading east, also watched. As I left, another rider did, too, then the last one fell in line. We were all headed for Riverside as the day grew warmer. We started a steady climb that continued for most of the rest of the afternoon. Our maps indicated that headaches, insomnia and shortness of breath were possible as the altitude increased. Riverside has camping and a motel, and some of the cyclists on the road had decided to use the afternoon as a rest day. I already had 62 miles and could have done the same. One of the guys who just left Saratoga had spent the night there and was going to ride the 48 miles to the next town. Some ice cream and a few Reese's Cups convinced me to join him. Actually, I left first because I was not interested in waiting to eat lunch.

The climb was constant, with an on-again, off-again headwind and some rain. I was headed for Walden, just across the Colorado line. In the meantime, I kept plugging. It was a hard afternoon. Traffic was light and I got to see a few rainbows, but otherwise my immediate goal was to make miles and find the Colorado line. Once I did find it, I took a photo. There was a man walking toward me who I later found out was hiking Colorado. We talked briefly and both kept rolling. This was going to be a long day.

My new friend still hadn't caught up yet. I looked back on occasion and didn't see him. Colorado roads immediately downsized to no shoulders at the state line and the surface was less smooth. I didn't know it at the time, but the quality of the roads in the first four states would be higher overall than any other state that I passed through heading east. I expected that Colorado's roads would surely improve. They never did.

Another thing about Colorado bothered me. Much of the state, except in the high mountains, was a series of low-lying ridges or berms. Many of the less-traveled roads, or most importantly the ones that are used by the TransAmerica trail, were for some odd reason paved so that the road went up and over, then down, then another up and over and back down. Climb, then recover at the top, then coast down, ride a half-mile of flat, and then climb again and just keep doing the same thing. The better roads ran between the ridges or had some grading to open up some continuity. Colorado was the one and only state that drove me crazy, and I am sure lots of other vehicle drivers the same. I found few roads that had been paved anytime recently-once again the worst of all the states that I rode through.

I made it to a little town called Cowdrey, home of not much except a liquor store, and then began riding up and over berm after berm after berm as I hoped to reach Walden before dark. Still no sign of my new friend, who had appeared to be a better climber than me. Finally, after a day that was longer in the saddle than any other, I rolled into town. I got a room at a motel, then ordered some food at the closest restaurant, all the while watching the incoming street. He rolled into town about 9:30 p.m., after dark, and cursing those endless berms. I submitted my daily story and went to bed. I had made 112 miles of moderate to heavy climbing. No day had whipped me physically more than this one, and no other day would for the rest of the trip. I was dreading what was left in Colorado.

After a short but restful night in Walden, I headed on out for the rest of the climb over the Willow Creek Pass at 9,621 feet in elevation. I stocked up at one of the local convenience stores, and left with a goal of ending the day as early as possible. My legs were tired after the high-mileage day yesterday but not enough to spend a rest day just ahead of this climb. Mentally, I needed something good to happen and part of my prayer that morning was for just that.

The climb was once again into a light wind, but not especially steep. After topping the mountain, I had a good bit of slow down-hill into Kremmling. With no shoulders again, I became so frustrated at one point with the traffic that I got off the bike and started walking in the grass. A motorist stopped and asked me if I was OK. I told him that I had a couple of close calls from traffic and he assured me that Colorado law requires all drivers to give cyclists a minimum of 3 feet of space. On a busy road, I know they may try to give that space but sometimes it just gets too tight. After a short time, I was back on the bike and riding into Kremmling, where I would get that "something good to happen."

I didn't have a room, but immediately saw several choices. I called the Hotel Eastin and found that a private hostel room was extremely reasonable, so I headed that way. The Van Lues had restored a 107-year-old hotel, but left much of the history intact. I checked in and was off the bike for the rest of the afternoon. That was exactly what I needed. Kremmling topped my list of top small towns. It was located at 7,500 feet and full of friendly people. I talked with Maryann Van Lue and found out more about the history of the hotel. It used to be a sarsaparilla factory, then was made into a hotel. Author Zane Grey wrote one of his novels here. The inspiration for his "Mysterious Rider" is an image on the canyon wall just on the edge of town. Doc Holliday was rumored to have stayed here. We talked about all this over cookies and tea. I walked around town for an hour and looked at all the history on hand. I sat down in the hotel courtyard and submitted my story for the day. I visited Subway and the local grocery store, one of my favorites on the whole trip. The grocery store has a recording of cows mooing that plays at regular intervals inside. Kremmling was a nice place to spend a long afternoon.

Back at the hotel, my friend from the day before had caught up again. His evening had not been as restful as mine, but at least he would get a good night's sleep in the Hotel Eastin. We headed for our rooms and I prepared for the biggest climb of the whole TransAmerica trail tomorrow. I would be going over 11,500 feet in the late afternoon on what would be another very challenging day. This had been just the afternoon that my legs needed. I felt ready to take on the Hoosier Pass.

I awoke early feeling great, but a little sad to be leaving the Van Lues and this wonderful old hotel. I headed out of town and began climbing. It was a cool morning to start. I found that nearly every morning in the high elevations would be cool, but then would warm quickly. Today ended up to be that kind of day, too. I pedaled through Silverthorne and Frisco. I had to ask for help in finding the route from Frisco to Breckinridge. Most of it was on a bike path that kept cyclists out of a heavily traveled road.

Famous fur trappers Jim Bridger, Kit Carson and Jedediah Smith had worked this area, just before three separate gold booms hit the town of Breckinridge. In 1860, 1878 and 1989, gold captivated the area. The early mining was done with placer mines, which involved washing sand and gravel through a sluice box. Later operations included dredging, which left huge piles of gravel in the area after separating dirt and rock from water. This was the same method used near Nevada City and Virginia City, Montana.

Today, Breckinridge is full of trendy shops and caters to a huge tourist influx. I had to walk my bike through parts of the town because the bike trail had ended and sidewalk and street traffic was extremely congested. Breckinridge served as the gateway to the Hoosier Pass. It also served as the last place to stock up on water and food for the final climb. I dreaded the climb itself, but knew that once completed, there would be lots of downhill for much of the rest of Colorado. I asked several locals for their estimates on how far to the top of the pass, and got responses ranging from 8½ miles to 15 miles.

There was nothing to do but get started on that final segment. I had been climbing toward this peak all day, and it was now mid-afternoon. It was time to push on toward the summit. The first 6-mile segment was a steady climb, most of it done in second and third gears. After passing through Blue River, I saw a sign that said four miles to the summit. Almost immediately, a series of switchbacks began that continued on with increasing tightness. After dropping to first gear, I couldn't balance the bike on the switchbacks with the steepness of the grade. I pushed the bike for the last part, which came quickly, and finally I was over the high pass. The snow line was just above me, as two more mountains on either side of the pass still had snow even on a warm day in July.

I topped the pass, and took a few pictures. Then a couple offered to take my picture and I did the same for them. At last, it was time for some downhill. Back on the road, I coasted and lightly pedaled for the six miles into Alma. Alma has a population of 270 and is at just over 10,000 feet in elevation. It was late in the afternoon as I rode into town. I quickly spotted a hotel named Alma's Only Hotel and stopped in to ask about their advertised hostel rooms. This was the start of the worst night of my whole trip, and it didn't take long to realize it.

Alma's Only Hotel just happens to be over a bar that stays open until 2 a.m. About six rooms share a bathroom that isn't serviced often, and it had been a little while since the last cleaning. I was shown a room that was OK, but wondered about the noise. I also wondered who would use the other rooms. I put my bike inside and then went out to get some food. The music and conversation level was already loud and getting louder. It was not going to be my night. The general store didn't have much of a selection but did have ice cream and some snacks. I ended up with a bag of Pizza Combos as the staple for my evening meal. Two ice cream sandwiches served as dessert. I sat outside and enjoyed watching patrons go back and forth between the two bars in town. That was until I realized that I had chipped a tooth while eating. After the general store closed, not another thing was open in town. I typed my newspaper story and submitted it, then headed for my room now since it was dark. No one else was in the hostel area. I got a shower and hoped to soon get some sleep. The shower was OK, but the sleep was fitful at best. As the night wore on, patrons of the bar gradually took the other rooms. Quiet didn't come until almost 3 a.m., less than three hours before I reloaded my bike and headed down the road. For once, I couldn't wait to get to get out of town.

Operating on little sleep, I still felt good. This morning was about to be one of the best memories from my journey. As bad for me as Alma was, I should have ridden on just a few more miles to Fairplay. I stopped for breakfast at the Brown Burro Café and didn't know what to expect, especially after the near sleepless night in Alma. Everyone in the Brown Burro, especially the staff, was extremely friendly. The waitress asked about my trip as I devoured great pancakes and eggs. The owner earlier told me to feel free to pull my bike up close to the door. Nearly every patron had something pleasant to say. I felt as if life were returning to normal.

One of the most interesting legends I have ever heard was the topic of some of the discussion that morning. I was told that Fairplay is the Burro Capital of the World. How that distinction got started is the most intriguing part of the story. Seems that a restaurant owner decided that the burro should be honored for all the work they do in mining, transferring equipment and ore. Just while this was going on, someone realized a burro that had recently died was lying in the town dump. Though this particular burro was probably only about 20 years old when he died, he was soon portrayed as having worked during the area's gold rush. This fabrication would have made Prunes the burro an impossible 63 years old at death. An old prospector was enlisted to validate the story and Prunes soon became a national hero. Tales soon came to light of his incredible intelligence and daring deeds. Prunes helped Fairplay become the Burro Capital of the World, and I was lucky enough to have breakfast there.

Just after leaving Fairplay, I began one of the best rides of my whole trip. Except for short intervals, most of the next 20 miles was downhill. It was a cool, crystal-clear morning. I rode by ranches in an area where lots of vacation homes were located. There was virtually no traffic, and I felt so small in God's creation. Huge mountains on my right were all snow covered, and I watched as the early-morning sun just touched on the peaks and then worked its way down. It was easy riding, allowing me to look at the scenery more than usual. This ride was a genuine "Wow!" moment.

The morning was one of the best, but the afternoon soon tried to make me forget that special morning. I had to cross one last high pass in Colorado called the Currant Creek Pass, listed at an elevation of 9,404 feet. Both the heat and winds were picking up, but still the long downhills were offsetting the winds. After crossing the pass, I quickly dropped another 2,000 feet for a total elevation decline of almost 4,000 feet in the same morning. I settled into a rolling ride as I headed toward Canon City, Colorado. Winds were now howling and I soon made a turn directly into a strong 30 mph wind. My quick pace soon came to a nearly grinding halt. I was on an uphill pedaling against the wind and down in the lower gears to do it. I was also low on water, having used more because of the rising heat. I thought of stopping at a campground as I slowly moved forward. This was one of the absolute low moments of the whole journey, and I hoped for a way to break through. I prayed to God, asking for His strength to be able to complete this segment and reach Canon City.

I kept pedaling for about two more miles, then noticed that the traffic was disappearing below the horizon in front of me. My prayer was answered as I got to that point myself and started a gradual downhill. The downhill grade offset the wind's worst effects and then as I continued downhill, the wind became less and less noticeable. It was at least a six-mile coast into the edge of town, but I was ready for the end of pedaling for the day regardless.

Canon City, another gold boom town, is another of my favorite places that I visited. It is historic and friendly, plus it has a scenic railroad headquartered right near downtown. I loved watching the engines exchanging cars and hooking up to other trains. My motel was right across from the train station. I checked in the motel, and decided to take a long walk to see the town. I found a recommended pizza and pasta place and settled in for a good meal that included a pizza and a complete order of garlic bread. I walked around some more afterward under a looming thunderstorm and found opportunities to eat two huge ice creams and two large brownies. Eventually I headed back to relax with a late-afternoon nap. My clothes got washed while I rested. This was a challenging day that ended with a total of 83 miles.

Through the night, I watched to see how much the wind was blowing and from what direction. For weeks, I had heard of the heat reaching the upper 90s and low 100s in eastern Colorado. I loaded up and left out early, hoping to beat the worst of the wind and heat. The first 20 miles were mostly downhill and the traffic was fairly light. I kept rolling, so much that I passed the proper turn in Florence and then ended up retracing my route slightly. I stopped in a grocery store parking lot to check my directions and got an interesting comment. A nice local man told me how to get back on the proper road, and then said, "So and so has built a castle just off this same road. It will only be about 12 miles off your course to see it." I thanked him for the directions and led with a huge smile as I drove away. On a day that would approach 100 degrees, I wasn't going to ride 24 miles out of my way.

On I went, climbing over Colorado berm after berm and passing uninspiring scenery. My map called for a store and restaurant coming up as the temperature continued to climb. I realized that with the lower altitudes there would be no need for my cold-weather clothes. I made a quick decision to ship my winter stuff back home at my first opportunity. By doing that, I could get more water and food in my bags. I came to the intersection that had the store, and found it closed and only open on the weekends. The restaurant was inside the store.

On I went with a developing tailwind that helped push me toward Pueblo. As I rode, the scenery turned to parched rangeland and high desert. Speaking of parched, that adjective soon applied to me, also. With just a few of the dreaded berms, most of the ride toward Pueblo went pretty well. I rode on and had to do some serious climbing to get to the center of town. I stopped at the first convenience store, and got plenty of water, another drink and some food. After asking the clerk where the McDonald's was, I headed there immediately for a second meal and some WiFi use. It was time to cool off.

My trip was nearing the halfway point. The guy in the Florence parking lot told me that once I left Colorado that I would hate Kansas. I was ready to leave Colorado, tired of the berms and ready to move on to another state. With its narrow and poorly maintained roads, I would like Colorado best when I last saw it in my rearview mirror.

CHAPTER 13
— Pueblo, Colorado to Alexander, Kansas —

Riding downhill across the high plains not easy

I'd had some long days in the saddle, and I knew that more of the same was on the horizon. I had been looking forward to eastern Colorado and Kansas, ready to leave the mountain climbing behind for a while.

Daily temperatures rose as I left Pueblo. My water bottles were full and I expected to need that much and more. After a long flat ride on Highway 96, my first stop was at a general store in Boone. I noticed that my water was getting warm in the bottles, but I had no idea of the actual temperature until Joanie in the Boone Grocery and Hardware told me that it was 102. About four days before, I had worn several layers of clothes during a 40-degree morning. I took the time to talk with Joanie as I enjoyed her air conditioning and ice cream. It would have been nice to visit longer, but I had a long way to go. Joanie assured me that the gathering clouds would not provide any rain because they were coming toward Boone from the wrong direction. I secretly hoped she was wrong, just to get a cooling shower.

I left Boone, with storms off in the distance, and terrific side winds began pummeling me. None of the big clouds produced any rain, though, so Joanie was right after all. This whole map was full of long stretches with little population. I saw Olney Springs listed as the next town, but there was not an open store in sight as I rode through. A few dogs didn't like the intrusion, though, and I did a few sprints on the bike as they tried to make closer contact with me. This was my first dog contact on the trip, but it certainly wouldn't be the last.

I kept rolling and ended a 104-mile ride at historic Ordway.

In an earlier phone call, Carol had promised me a good deal on a hostel room and I was ready for it. Just as at the Hotel Eastin in Kremmling, I was totally immersed in a time long past when I entered the door. I had a huge room upstairs with only me using the bathroom across the hall. It was warm in the room but there were fans and a huge window that would serve me well later. Carol told me that the choices for food were limited in the area, but a grocery store was on the next block. She said, "You had better hurry because it closes in about 20 minutes." I hustled over and bought up a bunch of cool produce, some cookies, several containers of yogurt and a huge container of ice cream. This had definitely been an ice cream kind of day. The store still had a few people in it at closing time, so I lingered to talk to one of the clerks about my ride. No doubt she knew I was a cyclist because I still had my riding shirt on, looked sweaty and spent, and was craving anything wet and cold.

Ordway would have made my list of favorite little towns, except that most of the buildings were vacant and there were so few people around. I found out from Carol that Ordway used to be a thriving town, relying on the railroad and a huge local produce business. Irrigation canals were in place that provided water to grow the produce. Eventually, the railroad left town and the town sold its water rights. Ordway did have a water park located right across from the hotel. It was intended for kids, but on this hot day at least one adult considered walking right into the water sprays and plumes. As the sun slowly set, I enjoyed my ice cream near the water park, occasionally letting the wind push a little spray toward me.

With few towns on the map, I went back to the room and made space for more water in my panniers. Now if I could just figure out how to carry ice cream sandwiches. The next few days were forecast to be extremely hot. I had to be mentally ready and take advantage of opportunities to fill the bottles. The cool days on the road were over and warm days would be the norm as I rode east. My cold-weather gear was ready for shipment home. I was officially over halfway now and excited by that.

Just as it was getting dark, the evening air started to cool. I opened the window and used my fans to make for a comfortable and restful sleep. Up early and ready to roll, I loaded my bike and spoke briefly to Carol's husband. He suggested that I consider stopping for breakfast at a restaurant in the next town. He promised me that I would never get a better cinnamon bun. He also told me that the town, Sugar City, was once nationally known for the area's production of sugar beets. With a tip on a shortcut back to the main road, I waved goodbye to Ordway and headed out of town.

I was still at over 4,000 feet in elevation, and there would be some more gentle downhills mixed in as I rode toward yet another sunrise. Upon entering Sugar City, I almost braked for the restaurant and even rode on by for about a block and circled back. Then I just kept going. The morning was just too cool to stop for a breakfast, so I vowed to push on and make the best of the day. I quickly noticed that a slight headwind was developing and as the sun rose, the intensity of that wind did, too. Visions of a good day soon began to disappear as the headwind was now the strongest that I had faced. A few hills and some of the last Colorado berms made the ride even tougher. Maintaining a speed of just 6 mph was now all I could do. Harwell, Colorado, was coming up and I hoped to refuel there and gain some momentum.

Harwell claims that it has the smallest jail in the world, probably because most of the population of 68 wouldn't come out in the heat to do anything bad. I pulled into the strangest little store, a cross between a tire shop, general store, a home and who knows what else. Nobody else was moving. Two adults and a child were lying on a couch watching TV and hardly looked up as I came in. I asked about ice cream, and was shown another interior door through which a freezer sat. The ever present Reese's Cups and some ice cream were among the minimal selection, so I could just make do. I asked about water and was told that I could use the outside spigot.

No need for anyone to miss your show on TV!

For the first time, small, biting flies harassed me. There was no place to escape them, except apparently on the couch with two industrial-sized fans blowing from each end. I quickly loaded up and headed out of town. Nobody noticed me leaving.

I kept plugging toward Eads, eventually meeting a cyclist on the road who told me that he was giving it all up after this day. I thought, "And he has the tailwind!" The winds were consistent and it was now just plain hot. Eads had a motel, and I could have stopped at about 60 miles with the hope that the wind would die down over night. Always the optimist, I kept pedaling even though I realized that my best hope for an end-of-day destination was still 30 miles away.

Several things began to appear in the seldom changing landscape. I passed long, extremely dry patches of land that looked unused on both sides of the road. Few cows or green sections were mixed in. I began to see quite a few small oil rigs, some running and some not. I classified this area as desolate, and expect few would argue. Needing something to laugh about, I envisioned the biting flies waiting near the road for the next cyclist to come by, mostly because they had no other place to go. My pace was slow enough that some of the biting flies didn't even wait for me to stop. They jumped on and started to bite even as I pedaled.

On I rode with my head down to avoid the wind's roar in my ears. Worse yet was when a cattle trailer would meet me on the road. I would be slammed with even more force by the upcoming wind. After passing through Chivington and Brandon, both with populations of less than 30, I focused on making the last nine miles to Sheridan Lake. The flies, heat and wind made for a miserable afternoon all the way around. In one of my happiest moments, I spotted the small town of Sheridan Lake on the horizon and rolled into the town's convenience store. As soon as I got off the bike, the flies followed and I just about ran into the store. That did little good because they were also in the store. I saw myself in a mirror and found salt streaks along both cheeks, just the same as if I had run a warm-weather marathon that afternoon. I wasn't sure that I didn't. Mileage today was 93, with the last 30 being the hardest segment yet.

Sheridan Lake was a small town, population 88, that revolved around the convenience store. I asked about a cyclist's hostel that was listed on my map. The clerk sent me to Sheridan Bible Church, just across the railroad tracks. She told me that the church always left a door open for cyclists and that I would like it. However, she also cautioned me to hurry back if I wanted some food before she closed the deli. I left with the flies in tow and promised to be back shortly. The church had a comfortable area with a huge kitchen, restrooms and plenty of room to relax. Another cyclist was already inside and he had just made an exercise of killing the flies that followed him inside. After unloading my bike, I hustled back over to the store and quickly returned with a pizza, some snacks and ice cream. While at the store, I found that the flies were a constant during the summer and that they were even more persistent this year. The clerk said that nothing seems to kill them. I simply couldn't imagine trying to avoid these flies all summer. So much for the old wives' tale that we need cold winters to keep the flies down, because this area regularly had winter temperatures below zero.

I also asked about all the land that seemed to be dried up and unused. The scenery here was non-existent, with hardly a tree in sight. After looking at the wasteland all day, I knew again that we were so lucky to have a more moderate climate back home in Rowan County. This area of eastern Colorado is the site of the famous Dust Bowl. During a huge drought in the 1930s, skies darkened as far away as New York City when furious winds blew the resulting dust into the air.

After a nice meal, plenty of good conversation with an experienced cross-country cyclist, and good night's sleep in the sanctuary of the church away from the flies, I was ready to roll early. Thankfully, I did not have to try to camp in the land of the flies. At this point, I would do anything to beat the wind that never totally rests in this area.

With an early start, I headed east again into a slightly less powerful wind. Still after 11 miles, I couldn't top 10 mph until after I found the Kansas state line. I was elated! Goodbye to the bad roads, and the berms and so much more. I crossed the state line on to a newly paved road, wide enough for a cyclist to ride on. The flies were still with me, but if reports from other cyclists were right, they would not be for long.

Almost immediately, the land started to improve. There were large fields actually being farmed, and big patches of green came into my sight. Especially interesting to me was the change of time zone. Mountain time does not change to Central time at the state line of Colorado and Kansas. The change actually occurs at the second county line. The heat continued to build, especially in an area where miles of new paving was being done. These people were friendly, yet professional, and certainly not involved with the group of pavers in the Grand Tetons who tried to keep me off the road. I actually enjoyed talking with the ladies who held traffic until the lead truck returned making it safe for us to pass through.

Grain storage facilities stood tall at regular intervals along the road. They are huge and can often be seen for as much as 10 miles. I found that I could focus on making it to one, then shift my focus to the next, and those mind games kept me going in the heat. I stopped in Leoti and had a convenience store late lunch. I realized that I was just across from a motel and called them to see if a room was available. I found that construction workers had the whole motel rented, leaving me no other option than to ride another 23 miles into the wind.

This 23-mile segment was best addressed by taking it in 5-mile segments. I began by rewarding myself with something to eat and drink after five miles, then cut it to three, and finally to every two miles. The headwind was at its worst in mid-afternoon. A sheriff's deputy asked me if I was OK, and I agreed that my efforts at pedaling probably looked miserable from the other side of the road. I was frustrated, dehydrated and hot.

Finally, I made it to Scott City, Kansas. With a pre-arranged room at the Plains Inn, I just needed directions and called to get them. Imagine how surprised I was to find out that the room was given to me for free since I was riding for the awareness of childhood obesity! I found the room, the door unlocked and waiting for me, and air conditioner humming at full blast. I loved the room and enjoyed a pleasant evening. Only a visit to the grocery store was worth leaving that room. I ate well and went to bed early.

It was hard for me to get out of that bed, but the wind and heat were slated to return. I knew that it had rained hard overnight and found a heavy metal chair blocking my door as I planned to leave. Weather forecasts said that huge storms were still around this morning, though none seemed close. I stopped in Dighton to get a couple of large, fresh cinnamon buns. They had become another high-energy favorite.

Kansas is not flat, but it was close enough for me to appreciate the fact that I was not climbing as much in the wind and heat. Scenery picked up, especially with lots of huge combines and tractors being hauled on the same roads that I was riding. During a visit to a truck stop, I heard a conversation about how many of the locals were away to help with harvesting in other states. Being a farmer, I appreciated these things.

After Dighton, there were a few more low hills that helped to deflect some of the winds. For just this one time, the hills served a good purpose. After about 10 more miles, the wind had picked up again enough that I chose to call it a day upon arrival in Ness City. Ness City was another of my favorite small towns, being both historic and friendly. My 2 p.m. arrival was early, but the temperature was already over 100 degrees. I got my motel room, and prepared my winter clothes for a trip to the post office. It was just a short walk, but just perfect to grab some ice cream on the way. I took my gloves and heavier clothes in to the post office, immediately setting off a group conversation. The helpful postal workers took a bag of my stuff, chose the right box, filled out the label and taped my box for shipment to North Carolina. In my opinion, if all post offices were this helpful and friendly, lots more smiles could be shared around increased business. Before I left, one of the customers quietly gave me a $1 coin, another smile, and a wish for good luck as I headed on east. It was hard to leave without a smile of my own. Today's mileage was only 58, but the early stop was the right thing to do.

In a rare long afternoon off, I watched my beloved Yankees playing the Kansas City Royals on TV, took a nap, and walked around town to see some of the sights. Ness City still has horse-tying hardware on the sidewalks and plenty of beautiful old buildings. This town is in the area where the famous cattle drives used to take place. Large herds of cattle were sent to Kansas from Texas for shipping to markets all over the country. Cattlemen and cowboys hold a revered place in this time, which they helped populate while adding to the folklore of the Wild West.

Right next door was an outdoor drive-through ice cream stand. I visited twice and felt refreshed by late afternoon. My plan was to go to bed early and get the earliest start yet on the heat and wind in the morning. I planned to be riding by 5 a.m., well ahead of daylight. As I headed for bed at just after 9 p.m., I noticed my front bike tire was totally flat. A flat tire in a motel room was much better than out on the hot roads, but I had to fix it that night. I changed the tube, and couldn't find any real reason for the flat, so I pumped up the tire. My mini-pump couldn't get the tire as full as I wanted, so I went out to the streets to see if I could find an air hose. After 9 p.m., nothing was open and I walked to both convenience stores to check for air. Disappointed, I started back toward the room and discovered a mechanic shop with a door open across the street. Turns out that the owner was there to prepare his boat for a day on the water, and he had air. In fact, his whole family was there, and his son actually offered the air hose for my use. It was another wonderful moment in which I could repair the bike and get back on schedule for the early departure next morning.

My 4:15 wakeup call never came, but I woke anyway at 4:19. My internal clock had improved quite a bit. A few quick bites from my packed food got me going, and I was soon on the road. Highway 96 that early morning had almost no traffic and I loved the early ride. The sky changed color right ahead of me from black to shades of blue, orange and red. This backdrop, joined with a gentle breeze, made my early ride enjoyable. Once the sun was up, I expected the wind to resume pounding me, and it did. A right turn to the south put the wind's full force squarely in my face. The next 30 miles would prove to be the hardest yet. My only driving force was the knowledge that a left turn later should shift the wind to the side. In the meantime, I knew the drill. My best tactics were to lower my head to reduce wind resistance and lessen the roar in my ears, and stop regularly to rehydrate. Short riding segments helped to make small victories. A nice conversation with a couple from Bolivia broke up the tedium. Sarah and Pedro were going to spend two years on the road, eventually ending in South America. I resumed the battle and soon found the hoped-for left turn. Now the strong wind wanted to push me into traffic as I caught its force from the right. As said before, I will take a side wind anytime compared to a headwind.

I pedaled on into Larned, Kansas, and another afternoon off. The early start had netted 65 miles against the wind, and that was enough for today. Physically, I was toast. I found the Townsman Motel with a special cyclist's discount and checked in with the temperature again over 100. There were very few trees here, except in the towns, and the land has become more rolling as I get closer to the Kansas-Illinois border. Larned is on the Santa Fe Trail, a trade route from Mexico north that allowed huge amounts of goods to travel reasonably between the US and its neighbor to the south.

On the last day in this segment, I rolled out again at 5 a.m. headed toward Alexander, Kansas. After asking directions, I headed out of town and couldn't wait for another sunrise. Long and hot riding had forced me to earlier starts, but those sunrises were so spectacular that they rivaled the lightning shows in Wyoming. Nature is so wondrous, yet few of us take enough notice of it. I passed through Alexander, Kansas in mid-morning, stopping for water as the heat was building.

Much of the ride in this portion of Kansas was an exercise in futility. Each day was hot, extremely windy and the scenery was mostly agricultural. I used little mind games to keep going. Some of those games came from my marathon experience. I did lots of math problems with my total mileage and pace, anything to keep my mind positive and active. Continuous pummeling from the wind and the hottest temperatures over the whole trip made this section a bicycling extreme sport. Never again would the wind or heat be this bad.

CHAPTER 14
— Alexander, Kansas to Girard, Kansas —

Moving toward improving weather

Heading into eastern Kansas, I knew that there was at least a possibility that the winds would lessen. The endless flatland was gradually coming to an end which should once again help with deflecting some of the heavier gusts. Another 5 a.m. departure made for one more beautiful sunrise and little traffic. It was easy to get used to this.

I was out of tubes, except for the one that had a slow leak. It would do in an emergency, but would then have to be changed shortly thereafter. A visit to a bike shop was in order.

In the low light of early dawn, I passed lots of agricultural fields. Most were irrigated with overhead systems and in fact many of them were running as I rode by. Few houses and farms were near the road, so I rode for 58 miles while looking at crops and a national wildlife preserve. There was no activity of any kind in the wildlife preserve, although a few water habitats were available to ride through off the road. No large animals were in sight, although I could hear lots of birds. Birds were fairly common in rural areas, so there was nothing to make me think they were especially concentrated in the preserve. I wondered if the wildlife preserve was like many of the National Park Service areas that I passed, succumbing to congressional funding issues. I saw several more glaring examples of this later.

After the 58 miles of riding with heat increasing, I was ready for ice cream. My first stop was in Nickerson, where a convenience store staff allowed me cold water for my bottles and a few minutes in the air conditioning. The ice cream worked its magic and I was on the way to Hutchinson, Kansas. I was about to turn south into what wind there was today, and with great pleasure I found it not to be an obstacle. Wide roads with good shoulders made my ride down the highway even better.

Once I reached Hutchinson, I headed for downtown and Harley's Bicycle Shop. They sold me two new tubes and I bought a handlebar bag, so I could do away with my dilapidated backpack. I couldn't wait to get that thing off my back so that my upper-body sweating would be reduced. The bike bag was like a small piece of luggage with various pockets, totally waterproof and, in my opinion, expensive. It had a perfect pocket for my iPad, another for my wallet and phone, plus lots of room for odds and ends such as lip balm (my lips had cracked terribly early on), toilet paper, change, snacks, etc. I later found out that the price was competitive with other models, and I was excited about using it right away.

When I travel, I have the habit of occasionally losing a few pieces of clothing. Usually I have no good idea where I lost them. Such was the case of my favorite dri-fit shorts. Gone but certainly not forgotten. After the bike shop visit, I headed on down to the local Goodwill and picked up a suitable pair for $3, then stopped for more ice cream at the Dairy Queen. I returned to Harley's to take a few pictures and get final directions on the hostel that I would use that night.

I talked briefly with the bike shop staff about Bob Dole having been from this area, and the fact that I was headed home to near Salisbury, North Carolina, his wife's hometown. Hutchinson, Kansas, is slightly bigger than Salisbury, although similar in appearance with lots of older homes and neat streets. I rode off to Zion Lutheran Church, the hostel where I would spend the night. The staff at Harley's gave me a key and instructions on how to get in. After finding the right door, I went in to check it out. Zion Lutheran is small, with the sanctuary right over a full basement below. The cyclist's hostel was in the basement, complete with mattresses, plenty of bedding, individual TVs over the bed, a shower and a huge kitchen. The church organist followed me in and introduced

herself as she turned on the air conditioning. The outside temperature was once again near 100 degrees and would still rise a few
more degrees before the sun began to set. I made my bed, brought
some of my gear inside, and then rode off to find some food and a
grocery store. The town was so nice that I rode around for several
miles, something that I almost never did. Friendly people, too, of-
fering directions and waving if I didn't need anything.

I got my groceries, once again using the Safeway/Kroger card for
a good savings. It had served me well from Oregon to Kansas. My
total TransAmerica mileage was 73 today, hopefully on the increase
as I envisioned the winds being less of a factor. Upon returning to
the church, I found that no other cyclists had come to the hostel.
It suited me fine to have the large basement to myself. Once again,
I wanted to be out quickly the next morning. It just happened to
be Sunday, and I knew that someone would probably be coming to
the church early. Fine with me, because I knew that I would be up
and gone.

Of course, good plans don't always work out. I had found an
alarm clock the night before and rigged it for a 4:15 a.m. alarm.
When it went off, I couldn't believe I had to get up already. Sleep,
as always in the churches, was very good. I ate, got dressed, but then
noticed that there seemed to be a flashing light in the windows. I
looked out the front door and found torrential rain falling, high
winds, and plenty of lightning. The storm cell was being shown
over and over on the local TV without any commentary. I lay back
down in the bed until 6 a.m., then checked again. Everything outside looked much better, although there was some flooding visible.
I got my bike, turned on the rear flashing light and headed down
the street. Near the edge of town, a tractor-trailer pulled by me in a
massive road work area and just barely cleared my handlebars. I had
been jolted awake for sure. Light rain continued to fall.

Headed for Newton on good road shoulders, I made moderate
time. The wind didn't blow much while the light rain was falling,

so I was hoping for more miles. A quick stop for a large brownie seemed to help and off I went, improving my time. Through 40 miles, all was well and I stopped for breakfast at a Subway. My map directions were hard to follow, so I asked two locals who in turn enjoyed asking about my trip. They gave me perfect directions, and told me, "There isn't much out there but a bunch of fields. A lot of our cyclists ride that road." Light traffic sounded good, but the scenery was uninspiring to say the least. Those local guys nailed it.

One more stop for some snacks to fill my bags and I headed out on their road. I dropped a Reese's Cup on the wet pavement, but quickly scooped it up within the required three seconds and immediately enjoyed it. The skies started to brighten, which made me cautious. I knew from farm work and running that the sun coming out often causes the winds to increase. That scenario occurred as the winds gradually picked up and were again pushing in my face. With the clouds and rain gone, the heat returned. To make matters worse, the hills also returned. Kansas was no longer even going to pretend to be flat. Those three factors combined to make the last 20 miles of a total of 77 tough. I met a foreign couple who were cycling east, and exchanged good information with them. They told me that there were no rooms in Cassoday, my intended overnight stop. They also said that the restaurant only had high fat, greasy stuff for sale, and there were no other stores.

The motel story is an interesting one. I had called Cassoday Lodging and left a message the evening before to inquire about rooms. The owner called me back to tell me that she had no rooms available, and didn't know of any residents who might rent one. I called again and told her that if she did get an opening to let me know, and after a period of no cell coverage, I found three messages telling me that I now had a room. When would I be there, and where was I driving from, she wanted to know. I called back and told her that I was a cyclist and would be there close to 4 p.m. I was assured that my room would be waiting for me. Being persistent paid off.

The worst hills were the last ones, but finally I rolled into the "Prairie Chicken Capital of the World." I rode through and didn't even see a town, and certainly no motel. I checked the address and pulled up to what looked like a 100-year-old mercantile store. It did not look like a motel, but as soon as I got off the bike, the owner came out and welcomed me. The old building was being remodeled, but the actual motel room was fantastic. Once again, the air conditioner was already on and cooling the room and soon after, a very hot bike rider.

The owner told me that the local store was open and had quite a few choices to eat, so I rode my bike about a mile to the store. There was a good crowd in the store and all of them were interested in my ride. I talked with them while eating some much needed ice cream, and checking out the menu. They had lots of sandwiches already made up in a refrigerator, so I picked out egg salad for my first one. Potato chips, another egg salad sandwich, and a few Reese's Cups would be my evening meal back in the room. I rode back without spotting a single prairie chicken and settled in to send my reports and have a relaxing evening. Suddenly, the motel started to shake as a huge train rolled by for about five minutes. I looked out and saw that the tracks were about a hundred feet away. Trains have always fascinated me.

I got set up again to write and the building began to shake again. Another long train rumbled by, and I soon realized that this would be the case for most of the night. Soon, I didn't even realize they were going by. An early shower, a movie on TV and a comfortable bed put me to sleep quickly. Cassoday was just fine, I thought.

Before going to bed, I added up my mileage totals. Since Astoria, I had pedaled 2,542 miles or about 62 percent of the total trip. My cross-country journey was planned to vary from the mapped version. Once reaching Damascus, Virginia, I wanted to find a safe and reasonable route back to home, then would pedal on to one of the nearby beaches to officially end the trip. At this point, I had about 1,600 miles to go. My pace was faster than I expected, with a daily average of about 74 miles a day, just short of the 77 I rode today. Today's high temperature of 88, well below the consistent 100s of the last few days, helped with that.

With no rest days so far, I knew that struggling to get up in the morning was a sign that I needed at least a part of a day off. Marathon training teaches a runner to be able to handle ups and downs, and there were lots of both on these recent rides. The town of Eureka had a couple of reasonably priced motels and some sights to see, so I considered pushing hard to make the first 40 miles and then re-assess my situation. My ride to Eureka went well and it was still not hot. Winds were rising, but at the present, still reasonable. I rolled into Eureka and got information on a restaurant and a grocery store. I saw the motel that I considered on the way in. Eureka had another fantastic grocery store, once again honoring the Safeway/Kroger card. I loaded my bags at the store, skipped the restaurant and decided to keep rolling. The rest afternoon could come later. I knew that eventually the weather would force a rest day.

Shortly after leaving Eureka, I spotted a group of four cyclists who were rather overdressed for the temperatures. They were parked on the other side of the highway, so I coasted over to them. They described themselves as a religious and nomadic cycling group. All of them wore several layers of light gowns and the men had long beards. Their leader happened to be in this group. He told me that they had a larger group farther back on the highway. He offered me some homemade energy bar as we discussed their approach to life. After leaving West Virginia, they stopped for a month to paint a house and had just spent a week camping in the area. He said that they probably would end up heading for California. I told them about my ride, and one of their guys told me that I definitely needed a rest day with all the Ozarks coming up. I thanked them for the food, wished them "Safe Travels" and headed on.

I started pushing on into some small hills and an increasing wind. All the towns for the next 50 miles were small. The next big town was Chanute, with several good deals on rooms, so I hoped it would be my final destination for the night. With a long ride to go, I stopped in Toronto, near the Cross Timbers State Park. This was another small town with a booming convenience store. I got my ice cream there and was asked to sign their cyclist register. I enjoyed talking with the attractive owner, who looked amazingly like a friend back home. The talk and the ice cream lifted my energy and I headed to Coyville. The road had some genuine climbs on it, the first I had seen in several hundred miles. Asphalt in the area was really poor, so I continually dodged big holes. The wind had decided to challenge me, and storms were forming in the area. I rode through Coyville, a surprisingly picturesque little town, and received lots of friendly waves. Coyville had a little park with a sign listing all the firsts over the years. Coyville was proud that it had the county's first hanging, right before saying, "Come again."

Just past Coyville, I met two brothers from Dallas heading west. Will and Graham were really pleasant, and we took some time to share information. The wind was a good tailwind for them on this particular road, and we laughed as I wished that one of the storms might come and cause the wind to change around and push me. Just five minutes later, the rain started to fall and the wind came around as a side wind. I rode on and made a left turn and amazingly, I now had a tailwind. I had forgotten how to handle it. No wind blowing in my face was a heaven-sent gift. Highway 38 and 2000 Road would take me the rest of the way to Chanute. The tailwind was really helping me and I enjoyed the rare treat to get into the high gears and run 15-16 mph. I got so excited that I totally missed the turn for the 2000 Road and had to follow Highway 38 on into Chanute. There were two things wrong with that. I added probably five miles to the ride, plus the last 10 were mostly a steady grade uphill. Upon entering town, I stopped at the first opportunity to find out where the motels were. I got a good deal on one, but the desk clerk couldn't tell me how to get there. Chanute was a large town for the area at 8,738 people and it seemed to take forever to pedal across it. Originally four smaller towns consolidated to form Chanute, possibly the reason for the oddly spread-out town. Good directions from a passerby on the sidewalk finally got me through town and to the motel. I found another perfect room to roll my bike into, and plenty of food choices were close by. My mileage total for the day was 100 even, a lot more than the 40 I earlier thought would have been enough. After eating constantly until about 9 p.m., I hit the bed and prepared for yet another early start. Missouri was just around the corner and I looked forward to it.

My motel was right on my route out of Chanute, so another 5 a.m. start got me rolling quickly. A four lane road with little traffic seemed perfect. Once again, taking something for granted was a mistake. I got four miles out of town and came to a road closed/bridge out sign. Not only was the road closed, but the pavement had been removed. The smooth, four-lane highway had been reduced to a rough dirt road, and I had no idea how to get around the road closed signs. It was still dark and I wondered who would be around to ask. Just up the road, I noticed an open door on a business with a couple cars sitting outside. Off I went to ask a way out of this dilemma. One guy tried to help me, but didn't know whether I could get across the bridge and another just suggested riding down to see if I could. The detour wasn't clear and part of it would be on gravel, not the best thing with a loaded bike. So I said yet another prayer and headed toward the bridge.

The bridge was a four-lane antique that looked like it was being replaced. There were huge gaps and unfinished parts of it, making any chance of crossing the bridge impossible. I looked underneath and realized that the drought had all but dried up the creek and I was able to get across it and proceed on toward my next turn off the highway. Another beautiful sunrise highlighted the morning. The two guys who tried to help me rode by in their van, waving as they passed. I had been lucky and blessed once again.

The road was now becoming more hilly, a predecessor to the Ozarks. Lots of short and moderately steep climbs worked me hard as I headed for Walnut. I had made good time all morning and stopped in to get a drink and spotted Little Debbie brownies, my favorites from home. While buying them and an ice cream sandwich, I talked to a local farmer about land prices, rental costs, rainfall amounts and other agricultural stuff. Land in that area of Kansas is still reasonably inexpensive, but it rents for more than I expected. It was fun to talk with the farmer and he told me where to watch for his farm as I passed. I was amazed to see so much huge equipment and lots of large, well-kept buildings to keep it in. Rain the night before had lifted the prospects of everyone in the area. Eastern Kansas had been in a severe drought. It was amazing that back home we had near record amounts of rain over the same time frame.

Girard, Kansas, was the last town in this section. I rode through a low traffic, farming area and covered the last 20 miles to Girard quickly. This area is all laid out in one-mile sections and easy to track distances. I rolled into the beautiful little town of Girard and completed Map 8 of the TransAmerica Trail. It had been a great day with no weather issues. The rides were becoming much more enjoyable.

CHAPTER 15
— Girard, Kansas
to Murphysboro, Illinois —

Riding through the Ozarks, a different type of hills

I was excited to get to Missouri. I enjoyed Kansas, but could have done with less wind and heat. However, I expected both, so there were no big surprises. Missouri, in addition to a lot of small, yet steep hills, was still going to be hot, but not oppressively so. Humidity would creep in and make a difference, especially after such a dry climate for most of the trip so far. First, I had to finish off Kansas.

After leaving Girard, I headed for Pittsburg, Kansas. I had talked with Bob at the Holiday Lodge the evening before and secured a room, expecting to arrive about 1 p.m. My plan was to push hard in the morning, then relax and recharge in the afternoon. The ride to Pittsburg was about 14 miles of rolling country, some through residential areas. I had seen few homes near the road in Kansas, so the scenery was definitely changing. With increased population comes the presence of dogs who want to chase after cyclists. This happened to me two more times on this day. I expected more dog encounters as I pedaled farther east.

Pittsburg is on my top 10 list of small towns. It has a population of just over 20,000. Virtually anything was available in town, but none of that was on my mind as I rode in. This was going to be my afternoon off. I had 60 miles completed for today and no thoughts of going farther. I walked into the Holiday Lodge at 12:55 p.m., and immediately Bob knew that I was the cyclist who had called earlier. After a short conversation about other cyclists who had recently stayed at his lodge, Bob told me that he would like to do something similar someday himself. Maybe a bike was not the best way for him, but he definitely wanted to see America.

I closed the curtains in my room and had a good nap. Then I walked over to the Walmart and picked up a few things, and ate two meals. Few people would know what I felt when just shortly after eating a full meal, I was ready for another one. On this day, I did just that. It was the perfect way to regroup and get ready for the next day. I knew I would be ready to go at full speed after an easy afternoon — in fact the most relaxing afternoon of my trip. I talked with Bob again later and told him that I was leaving really early the next morning and would probably miss him, and then just a few minutes later, he brought me my breakfast so that I wouldn't miss that, too.

My early departure went well. I had no trouble getting out of bed for the first time in at least a week. The anticipation of meeting the Ozarks for the first time helped boost my energy. My goal was a long day's ride after the afternoon of rest. My first 30 miles went well, especially with crossing into Missouri and seeing another spectacular sunrise. I knew the hills would be starting soon, and they did. The expected humidity was a part of the mix, as was the low-lying fog near daybreak. It was certainly another hot day, and I needed a place to refill my water bottles with cold water. Out in the middle of farming land was the biggest farm equipment facility that I had seen. I pulled my bike over and leaned it against a line of all-terrain vehicles, then walked inside. Apparently, I wasn't the only cyclist who had visited this place. I walked into the middle of salesmen and farmers, and several office workers going about their business. One of the office staff smiled and walked over to tell me where the water, restrooms, drinks and snacks were. Instead of feeling out of place, I quickly felt at home. They didn't have ice cream, though.

Back on the road, I headed for Golden City, Missouri, listed on the map as having all services. When I got there, my map had me turn right before entering the town. I felt OK and was making pretty good time, so on I went. Everton was the next town, but off the route slightly. I did stop at Ash Grove, with already 72 miles covered and uncertain of a plan for the rest of the day. There was a cyclist-friendly convenience store, complete with a dry-erase board of all the cyclists who had stopped in recently. I loved it when the owner said, "Go ahead and fill your bottles with ice, too." Cold water was always better than hot, particularly when tackling these hills. I sat outside and considered briefly that this might be a good place to end the day's ride. But I simply felt too good, and quickly ruled it out. An unlikely visit with a local cyclist provided lots of information. After he asked about my ride, I asked him what the road would be like ahead. He described it in complete detail and exactly what to expect in each of the towns. From his description, I planned to find a good place to camp, unless I could really make some miles during the afternoon. We developed a different route from my map, and I was confident enough to take it.

This would be the first time that I made a significant route change from the one suggested by Adventure Cycling. It would not be my last. I never got the local cyclist's name, but I should have. I rode toward Williard on a hilly road that would only last about eight miles, and then turned toward Springfield, Missouri. I followed a busy four-lane road, all the time with a wide and well-kept shoulder. My directions called for riding to Springfield, then jumping on the old Route 66 before heading north toward Marshfield. My mind started to spin and I saw that Interstate 44 also went directly to Marshfield from Springfield. Wind was not a factor this afternoon, and I did not miss it. Finally, a whole day without the wind!

I pulled into Springfield with 90 miles already complete for the day and asked if there was a law against bicycles on the interstate in Kansas. No one in a convenience store had heard of one, and one guy was adamant that it was OK. He said, "I would do it if I was you. It is the best road around and no big hills." I loaded my bottles, ate four Reese's Cups and pedaled up the ramp. I was off to Marshfield. Traffic was heavy as I was right in the middle of rush hour. I still had my full lane to ride in, and the only time I had to worry was when passing an off or on ramp. A heavy rainstorm hit the area about 15 miles from Marshfield, but nothing else slowed me down. Finally at just around 7 p.m., I exited the interstate into Marshfield. I had made a total of 116 miles, but a few interesting things were yet to happen before I left the next morning.

I stopped at one of the busy gas stations and asked where the particular motel was. One lady told me it wasn't at this exit and a guy told me that he had never heard of it. I called the motel and the owner said, "Just keep going, you will see it. Look for the big green awning." I rode on and realized that nothing looked right and asked again, and finally rode back to where I first stopped. There it was! Turned out the motel was right beside the interstate and easy to spot. I got checked in, but the owner didn't want me to put the bike in the room unless I put a sheet of cardboard underneath it. That was fine with me, but she actually had to place the sheet herself and then watched to make sure I put the bike on it.

I rode later down to McDonald's to submit my newspaper update and a local resident walked over to ask if I was going to ride any more that day. I told him that I was not, and assured him that I was soon to be in my motel room. He told me that another long-distance cyclist, a female, had been hit in the early morning just a few days before. The resident's friend had been the one who hit her, and was distraught by the accident. The rider remained in the hospital after being knocked into the ditch. All of this happened in the dark before dawn. Add to this the news that a male local cyclist was killed in the Ash Grove area recently, and I assessed my habit of leaving well before dawn. I felt sure that the extreme heat of Kansas was probably less of a factor for the rest of the ride. I decided to wait until at least there was some light in the sky, especially when I would be traveling on roads with significant traffic.

Back in the motel, I felt great, even with the day's long mileage.

Only a third of the trip remained. While watching the weather on TV, I realized that the high temperature was 96 in Springfield. It just didn't seem that hot. Regardless, I still planned to delay my start in the morning. The Ozarks lay in front of me. They cover about 40,000 square miles and are considered one of the oldest mountain ranges in the world. The Ozarks are the only mountain range between the Rockies and the Appalachians. I knew that westbound cyclists all talked about how tough they are. I had to cross them to finish the journey, but at this point knew that I could handle the ride.

My delayed departure kept me at the motel until about 6:30 a.m. I pedaled out of the motel lot and on past McDonald's. Just on the other side of Marshfield, I heard an unusual noise from the rear tire. The tire looked fine, but was making a scraping noise. I looked back again and realized that nearly all the air was out of it. The tire had to be repaired, and thankfully after the stop in Hutchinson, I had tubes. Once again, I unloaded the panniers and laid everything out on the ground. I sat down on the ground and went to work on taking off the wheel, then taking out the flat tube, and finally replacing that tube with a new one. On this trip, I didn't waste time trying to find a hole and patch it. It was quicker and more reliable to put the new tube in right away. After pumping up the tire again, and reloading my bags, I stopped at one of the local convenience stores with free air to top it off. At 7:30 a.m., I was ready to roll.

The Ozark hills were never-ending on the road from Marshfield to Hartville. After 30 miles of riding, and most of the morning gone, I pulled into Hartville to discover that yet another bridge was out on my route. The local residents were happy to tell me how to get around it, and everyone seemed in a good mood. I stopped at the last convenience store for a few snack items, and was able to watch a domestic dispute across the street. It was better than TV, but finally a car arrived to pick up the man and the show was over. Maybe everybody was not in a good mood! I rolled on out of town.

Hill after hill, some steep, some not, but they kept coming. There was more climbing than downhill, so I knew my elevation was increasing. Next stop was a town called Bendavis, but it only appeared on the map as a town. Not much was there. The convenience store had cheap ice cream, perfect again for another warm afternoon. I sat down to talk with the owner for a few minutes. He wanted to know why I would want to ride so far on a bike, and I gave him my reasons. The store had almost nothing in it, and the water was terrible. I figured it was better to keep drinking my warm water than refill it with something that tasted so bad. Another customer came in, and I took that as my cue to hit the road.

The Ozarks don't have spectacular views because the mountains are not high compared to the Rockies or Cascades, but occasionally, there would be some great scenery. I passed a fire tower and knew that I had to be near the summit of the mountains in this area. A fire tower is the place from which fire spotters keep an eye on the forests, hoping to get help for any fire before it becomes a major event. Two more towns, Fairview and Bucyrus, didn't notice me as I pedaled on by. My goal was Houston, Missouri, and that is where I spent the night after climbing three of the worst hills all day to enter the town. Houston had a McDonald's and a Walmart, a rarity in these parts. It must have been a "real town."

After learning from the locals that the next day's climbs would be the worst of the Ozarks, I planned yet another early start. Some of the best scenery was reported to be near here, along with a good dose of Civil War history. Granite rock at the core of the Ozarks was only exposed on the eastern side of the range, and my maps said I would see lots of it. Several folks had warned me that the climb over Pilot Knob would be brutal. I went to sleep worried.

Up and out early, I pushed on with little traffic but lots of Ozark hills. The morning was a little cool, but after about 30 miles, the only thoughts of anything cool centered around ice cream. After

122

passing through Summerville, I headed for Alley Springs. I was now in the Ozark National Scenic Riverways and hoped to a see a lot of water. Alley Springs was supposed to be a haven for tubers, and certainly lots of their vans and trailers were on the road. Still, it was a big letdown to see a nearly dried-up river with an overload of tubers just trying to get their feet wet. A newly paved wide road was my reward that morning as the climbing and the heat both were building. Every time I climbed a hill, the only reward at the top was the sight of another one. With the heat up and all of this repetitive climbing, I began to sweat profusely. When I wore a short sleeve dri-fit shirt, the sweat would constantly drip off my elbows. I kept looking for scenic waterways but never saw a one. Just more hills.

My destination for the evening was Ellington, Missouri. I had anticipated picking up a package at the post office, one that was shipped from the Sock Guy in Carlsbad, California. The Sock Guy provides socks for all manner of athletic events, especially running and cycling. Ken DeCesari had found my journey updates online and sent me a care package of much-needed items. By checking online, I knew that I had to be at the post office window before 4 p.m. to make the pick-up, so I headed directly there. I spoke with the postmaster and a local guy who both had plenty of recommendations for me, especially for the best ice cream in town. The motel room was calling my name, and I headed that way with my care package secured to the bike.

Once in the room after 72 challenging miles, I found that the box contained plenty of socks, a cycling shirt, two pairs of high-quality cycling shorts and plenty of Clif bars. Along the way, all of my socks had taken a beating. Good socks will wear out in the friction spots, and my last pair already had one hole in them. One pair particularly caught my eye. Black, with green four leaf clovers on the ankles, and very comfortable. They quickly became my favorite socks and lasted the rest of the trip. The Clif bars lasted about two days.

At home, I have never been a big fan of air-conditioning and only use it sparingly. Yet after all of these hot days, I really appreciated it. Often the motel air-conditioning was too chilly for me and I would cut it down after getting cooled off. I got used to summer heat early in childhood while living on a small dairy farm and have always preferred hot days to cold ones. That preference worked out perfectly for the last half of the TransAmerica crossing.

Ellington made my list of top 10 small towns. Every person I talked to was helpful, especially the waitresses at Spooner's, a throwback dairy bar that had a big following. I kept going back myself, and ordered there three different times. I knew I liked it when I walked in and the jukebox was playing "Honey" by Bobby Goldsboro, and a couple of teens were singing along. Down the street at the Dollar General, I replaced my wallet that had fallen apart that day. The clerk made the purchase enjoyable by telling me about the varied wallet selection. They had the same wallet in two different colors.

There was plenty of Civil War history in the Ellington area. Both sides had strong factions locally and armies from both sides campaigned close by. The Confederates burned the Ellington courthouse, even though Missouri was considered a slave state at the start of the war.

After another good night's sleep, I headed out early again with the hope of making a stop later at a bike shop in Farmington. My bike was making a few noises, and I needed to get them checked out. Scraping sounds in lower gears didn't make me confident. Those gears made a few noises as I climbed a significant hill out of Ellington, one of the longest and worst of the day. Maybe this was a good thing, because the hills seemed more reasonable later that morning, or maybe I had become a little better at taking them on. During the morning, I stopped at Centreville for a small snack and a little conversation. About 30 miles later came Graniteville, not much more than a booming convenience store. My first ice cream and a chance to watch customers — a perfect break.

While studying my maps, I saw that the TransAmerica route went the long way around to Farmington. Convinced that I still had plenty of time to make the bike shop, I stayed on the route. It later turned out to be a good choice. After a long downhill on Highway 21, I wanted to make sure to see the Civil War battlefield in town, known as Fort Davidson, crucial in blunting the Confederate advancement early in the war. It was nice to see a well-maintained battlefield and museum, staffed with park rangers and volunteers. I already knew that U.S. Grant, eventually the commanding general of the U.S. Army, was posted in this area as his first command. The rangers told me about some sights to see concerning Grant, but it would mean backtracking, and I didn't want to chance it. I needed to get to the bike shop, so I made a quick tour and then hit the road.

Several cyclists had told me how hard the upcoming climb over the highest part of the Ozarks was. I wasn't disappointed to find a nice shoulder for virtually the whole climb and seemed to have plenty of momentum to get over this last mountain before Farmington. In fact, I only used my granny gear briefly before topping out and starting a long downhill toward Doe Run and then Farmington itself. As happened on occasion, I wondered if I was on the right road because there were no signs and little traffic. I found a mechanic shop open on this Saturday afternoon and walked the bike over some big gravel to ask. The owner's whole family was there and they all assured me that I was on the right road and would see some signs shortly. They offered me cold water and plenty of good wishes as I rode away.

Doe Run was the next town, but I didn't stop. A huge thunderstorm was building to the south and with Farmington less than five miles away, I wanted to be in the bike shop by the time the rains came. I climbed a few hills both in Doe Run and upon entering Farmington. The bike shop was in the downtown area and easy to find. Just before the first drops, I found Trans Am Cyclery and asked for a couple of tubes and a checkup on my lower gears. The owner looked at the bike and said it looked fine. He also fixed my mini-air pump that had come apart. The best part of our conversation was concerning the local cyclist's hostel that I hoped to find shortly. I was amazed that it was right across the street, and I didn't need to call the police to get in. It was great to leave the bike shop with so much information and only a short walk to get in one of the most interesting hostels on my route. The Town of Farmington closed their historic jail and made it a cyclist's hostel. The downstairs had a spot to store bikes, and the upstairs had been renovated with bunks, a kitchen, bathrooms, showers, laundry and a TV area. Just as soon as I arrived, the thunderstorms sent a huge downpour and heavy winds. Lots of tree damage and some flooding brought out the town street department for cleanup late on this Saturday afternoon.

My mileage for the trip now totaled 3,002, after a final total of 62 for the trip to Farmington. Warm weather replaced the cool, wet weather that I saw six weeks ago along the Oregon Pacific coast. The Mississippi River was now on my mind. I knew that I would be headed home when I saw the mighty river.

I had the streets to myself as I left Farmington, Missouri early on Sunday morning. A cool and drizzly morning with some fog in spots obscured the sunrise, but that was OK because of the pleasant temperatures. The maps told me that the worst of the climbing was over for Missouri, although a few challenging hills remained. There were nice views of surrounding farmland and a good selection of churches preparing for services. I found a convenience store in St. Mary and stopped for a short break and some food. Signs along the walls of the store said, "Cyclists, please do not lean your bikes against the store." Most of the better touring bikes, mine included, don't have kickstands. Cyclists have to find a place to lean them, preferring not to lay them down. My bike ended up leaning against a little bait storage area. I wondered if the signs meant that the owner was not especially happy to have cyclists stop in, but I found her to be friendly. I confirmed directions and set out to go find Illinois.

Just after a few tough climbs out of St. Mary, the surrounding land suddenly became flat and heavily agricultural. Field after field of beautiful corn stalks lined both sides of the road. The Mississippi was getting close. Just a few miles later, I saw signs for the bridge that would take me over the river and into Illinois. Traffic wasn't particularly heavy as I crossed the river, so I stopped on the bridge to take a few photos even though signs said "No Stopping on Bridge." Nobody seemed to care, and I cruised off the other side of the bridge and pulled over at the welcome center.

As I arrived, a cyclist heading west joined me. Chuck Walker was one of the most interesting characters that I met on my journey. He was from Maryland, but had worked in law enforcement in California until retirement. Chuck was extremely personable and we talked quite a while. I noticed that he was using an actual road map instead of the TransAmerica maps. I told him about the jail hostel in Farmington, but knew that he would have to hustle to get there. Chuck told me that he was traveling cross country because he had lost his faith in Americans, and hoped that this trip would give him some hope that our great country was going to survive. I had not lost my faith in Americans, but I was distressed about some of the things that have gone on recently. My goal was to meet lots of good people, down to earth, hardworking folks that I would like to spend some time with. That goal had been greatly exceeded so far. Chuck was one of them. He and I shared e-mail addresses and vowed to keep in touch. I heard from him after I finished my ride that he was on the way back to California and was doing well. I also told him that I would check in with him once he completed his journey. I hoped he would have lots of good stories about the Americans who are worthy of his trust.

There was a long climb from the Mississippi River Bridge to downtown Chester. I rode through and confirmed my directions. My plan was to ride the river levee for most of the afternoon through some small towns, then turn my sights on Murphysboro, Illinois. I caught a few sights of the river early on, and saw some beautiful agricultural areas with more giant corn. The spring and summer had been good for growing corn locally. I stopped at Todd Wilburn's antique shop to get a drink, and ended up talking about lots more. Before we parted, Todd gave me some landmarks to look for while seeking Sand Ridge, the last little town and final turn before Murphysboro.

I got to town, took care of things, and settled in with my feet up to watch some baseball and listen to a rainstorm outside. As the days passed, one of my biggest pleasures remained my quiet time after the day's ride and submitting my update to the paper. I caught up with messages from home, and I studied my maps, wondering about what the days ahead might bring. Today, I was focused on Kentucky and my route to get there. I didn't feel rushed to figure out the best route because Adventure Cycling usually does well with that, but after listening to those who have been on multiple trips, there is nothing wrong with analyzing the routes. Sometimes the mapped route is close to a point of interest worth seeing. Soon, I would encounter this scenario.

CHAPTER 16
— Murphysboro, Illinois to Berea, Kentucky —

Rolling hills throughout and some interesting characters, plus plenty of history

Never-ending hills dominated this part of the route. I was excited for the opportunities to see significant points of history. I have always loved history and found myself willing to go off route to see new things.

My ice cream addiction had taken over my body. With the Rockies long gone, nobody in this area had heard of huckleberry ice cream. My new favorite had become Blue Bunny's Strawberries Are Forever Shortcake ice cream. The heat was less than in Kansas, but the humidity had been building once I crossed the Mississippi. Every stop for ice cream helped recharge my body, especially my legs.

My route out of Murphysboro, Illinois went slightly off the TransAmerica map for the morning ride. The motel owner gave me some great advice. I used Highway 13 to get to Carbondale, pop. 25,000, and the biggest town that I would see in Illinois. I kept rolling on good shoulders, some of the best of the trip.

My goal for later this day was to make Cave In Rock, the last town in Illinois. I had called a motel the night before and the owner told me that if I could give her my time of arrival, then she could be there to check me in. That sounded just a little unique, but I pedaled on in hopes that things would go well. A cool and cloudy morning made my pace better than expected. More and more trucks were on Highway 13 as I neared my turnoff toward Cave In Rock. I didn't worry because I had a shoulder to ride on. I left the highway and turned on State Road 1. The motel owner had told me, "From the direction you are coming, there are only two little climbs." I was excited about that statement all morning but disappointed to find no less than 14 gut-wrenching low-gear climbs. As I have said, perception in a car is way different than on a bike.

While I struggled toward Cave In Rock, I met Edward Mjelde. He was walking across the United States, hoping to inspire others to get active. He was in no real hurry and planned to take up to two years for his journey. We talked for a while on the side of the road as the trucks whizzed by, then exchanged photos and headed our separate ways. There were more and more trucks and I had no idea what they were hauling or where they were going. None were in sight when I finally made it to Cave In Rock. Just before the main part of town, I passed the motel. It was just mid-afternoon and there was more energy left in my legs. I was worn down a little from 82 miles already, but there were two restaurants in the little ferry town that sold ice cream. I inquired about the road on the other side of the river and was told that it was hilly but not too bad. By this time, I knew that although well intentioned, that description was just about useless.

I saw the ferry loading for the short trip over the Ohio River. It was too late for this trip, so I headed to the restaurant to get ice cream and ice water. The ice cream was expensive, yet good. I had a few bites as I waited in line to board the next ferry crossing. The temperature had climbed into the upper 80s as I followed about 10 vehicles of all descriptions up on the ferry and enjoyed the ride across a scenic river. When I arrived on the other side, my ice cream was gone and I was ready to ride 12 miles to Marion, Kentucky, my new destination for the night.

The ferry crew unloaded all the vehicles first, then let me walk the bike off the ferry and up the ramp on the other side. The next load of cars and trucks had to wait until I was out of the way, but no one seemed upset. Several waved as I pushed by. The total ferry ride was about 15 minutes, a wonderful interlude between some hard pedaling that finished off Missouri and more needed as I entered Kentucky for the first time.

Just off the ferry and out of the way of traffic, I heard someone hollering, "Hey, do you have a dollar?" I looked over and saw a heavily bearded man and a teen standing behind a box. The bearded man introduced himself as Mountain Man. He said, "I have something here that only a few people have ever seen and if you have a dollar, I will let you see it. Just hold your dollar and look at it, and if you think seeing this thing was worth a dollar, then you can give it to me." I asked him if I could take a picture and he agreed that I could if I gave him the dollar. What I saw looked like the mounted head of a cat with large teeth connected to a lobster's body, one of only two of these in the world according to Mountain Man. I gave him the dollar and made my photo and was glad to do it.

Then Mountain Man told me that he had plans to be lowered into the Ohio River in September. His body would be in a closed and chained casket, lowered from a crane, and his only chance was to get out of the casket before he drowned. Mountain Man told me that his wife didn't want him to wait until September. He said, "She told me that I should go ahead and do it now." With that I said thank you and headed on into Kentucky.

The ride to Marion was not too hard, although it had some hills on blind curves. I immediately knew that there wouldn't be a lot of traffic because the Amish used the road for horse-drawn travel. Most of the traffic that I saw was either coming off the ferry or headed toward it. While waiting for the ferry, I had called a cyclist's hostel at the United Methodist Church in Marion. The secretary gave me the pastor's cellphone number and said that she would be gone when I got to town, but to call the pastor no matter the time of my arrival.

Pastor Wayne Garvey answered my call right away and gave me directions to the church. After 96 total miles for the day, I was ready to get off the bike. Pastor Garvey met me at the door and we walked the bike up a set of steps into the large church building. He told me that the church had a long-standing tradition of helping out long-distance cyclists. We talked a while and then he showed me the shower, several bathrooms, a huge kitchen and a room with couches and chairs where I could sleep. Soon, I had the building to myself. After a walk to get a huge meal and some more food for later, I headed back to the church and read notes from many of the recent cyclists who had stayed at the church. This had been a good day and I expected a good night's sleep.

Just about every day on the road, I had long stretches of time with uninspiring scenery. Long hours on the bike meant that something had to occupy my mind and lend to the overall effort. At various times, certain songs would begin to play over and over in my head. While riding through this part of Kentucky, I had two that helped me either pass the time or pick up the pace. One of my favorite songs of all time is "My Old Kentucky Home," written by Stephen Foster in Bardstown, Kentucky. Nothing is better than the exciting Saturday afternoon in May when the Kentucky Derby takes center stage. Foster's ballad is sung by the crowd as the horses head for the starting gate. I planned to see Bardstown later the next day. Jerry Reed's tune "Eastbound and Down, Loaded Up and Truckin'" seemed to be a good match for my pedaling cadence when I needed a boost. This song probably didn't have anything to do with Kentucky, but I liked it anyway.

I had another great night's sleep in the church in Marion. I got up refreshed, more than most mornings, following a habit of often being able to fall into a peaceful sleep in church. My former wives and girlfriends would probably agree, because I have been punched a few times during Sunday morning services. Just before leaving, and the usual prayer, "Ride with me today, Lord," I decided to make this day a slightly shorter ride and take advantage of another free hostel that night.

Off I went through lots of beautiful farmland. There was towering corn on both sides of the road as I passed through Dixon and Clay. I pushed the pace fairly hard, yet stopped for ice cream and Reese's Cups in Beech Grove. The convenience store clerk gave me a free Kentucky map so that I could better plan the next few days. Kentucky had lots of history that I wanted to see, but I would have to leave the planned route to do it.

Utica, Kentucky, had a fire department that was especially friendly to cyclists. I had a rather comical experience as I entered town, which was not much more than a crossroads. I asked one resident where the fire department cyclist hostel was, and he told me to turn left and ride up the main road just a quarter of a mile. Looking hard as I went, I didn't see anything that looked like a fire department, so I turned around and rode back down the same road. I spotted a guy who was just starting to mow his yard. He was ready for an afternoon in the sun, wearing shorts and slathered in sunscreen. I pulled in to ask him where the fire department was. He didn't slow the motor or stop the blade while I asked, so he sprayed me with grass. He pointed across the road at a building and said, "That's it," just as he drove away. End of conversation. I rode over and looked at the building, clearly designated with a construction company sign. I was bewildered until a little girl who was selling produce next door told me that it wasn't the fire department anymore. Her mother told me to ride back down to the crossroads and take a left and I would see the fire department. She was right, and I wondered why there was so much confusion about the location.

The Utica Fire Department was almost new, and I was impressed that the firefighters leave the door unlocked for cyclists. I walked in and found a large sleeping area with a couch and floor mattresses. There was a nice kitchen, a good shower and a washer and dryer. I needed desperately to give my cycling clothes a good washing. Another trip out to the convenience store for food and a visit to the Dollar General for some laundry detergent filled part of the afternoon. I quickly went back to get cleaned up and write my story of the day for the newspaper. A good shower never felt better and I put on clean clothes for the first time in several days. Next, it was back to the convenience store to use their WiFi to submit my story and order a pizza. I was all but done for the day, and settled in early to watch a lightning show that went on for hours through the large windows of the fire department. Once again, no other cyclists came in. Just like most of the other hostel accommodations, I didn't have to share the facility. I made 72 miles for the day, and had a relaxing afternoon. This was another good day.

Speaking of other cyclists, I had seen few as I got closer to the end of my ride. I checked the log for other cyclists who had used the fire department hostel, finding less than one a day on average. I am not sure that many of the cross-country cyclists actually travel through the Ozarks or the southern Appalachians. Earlier, I had met a large group and at least one individual that bypassed the area. Eastern Kentucky and Western Virginia are the gateway to the Appalachians, and tough.

I slept eight hours that night, probably for the first time on the whole trip. I don't usually sleep that much, but needed it this time. As I packed up, I noticed the flag outside had changed direction and now blew from the north. The slight breeze was cool, a pleasant change as I pulled away to head east toward Whiteville, Kentucky.

Today's route was more challenging based on my maps. Whiteville was just a 20-mile ride through some of the best-kept countryside that I had seen lately. Whiteville itself was more of the same, and made my top 10 list of small towns. The IGA grocery store was well stocked with usable groceries and pleasant workers. I stopped there and immediately struck up a conversation with some nice people who kept a log of cyclists who stopped. I stocked up on groceries for the first time in several days, and stayed to eat my breakfast outside. The extra space in my bags was now filled with bananas and cookies, plus a few energy bars. There were some good buys on Reese's Cups, too, so I took advantage. They only last a few minutes in the hot weather, but they would hold together for much longer on a cooler day.

Next town was Fordsville but I rolled on to Falls of Rough. The real climbing for the day was about to begin, so I stopped for a short break at the only store in town. My bike gears were making a popping noise again, so I asked if they had any machine oil. They didn't, but I got the scoop about the area from Bruce, who has a vacation home there. He told me to watch out for traffic, but the roads would be OK. He was right about the roads, other than some challenging hills early, and I just kept plugging through McDaniels and Madrid. I felt a little guilty stopping for ice cream late in the day. A day with a high temperature around 85 was so nice compared to the hot days of Kansas and Missouri. Pleasant houses and small farms made up most of the landscape.

I headed for yet another hostel, this one called the Double L Shop. It was at a road intersection, but not in a town. Another cyclist had recommended it to me, so I pulled in the parking lot of what looked like an old gas station. Pumps were disassembled outside. I wasn't sure this was the right place until I stepped inside. I got mixed responses from those inside when I asked if I was in the right place. The owner even smiled as he shook his head no.

The Lucas family readily took me in and showed me around the store, even though they were headed out to take care of some family business. They made me a couple of grilled cheese sandwiches and made sure I had a shower before they left. Just as they were about to go, Mathias Erb from Germany rolled in. This time I wouldn't be the only person in the hostel. Mathias had just finished school and took three months and a 90-day visa to bicycle across the United States. He was a lot of fun, and we had a nice, long talk while sending messages and my updates on the Lucas family's WiFi. We both chose to sleep outside under an overhang. The evening got cool quickly and we were in our sleeping bags shortly after dark. Mathias told me that he just couldn't get up early in the morning, but

I suggested he would have to consider doing so to beat the heat of Kansas and eastern Colorado.

Today's cool temperatures had kept me from feeling too tired, so I was excited about the next day's travel. I had crossed into the Eastern Time Zone and totaled 73 miles that day. There was lots of tobacco growing beside the road for the first time on my trip. I noticed an interesting church in Pleasant Point that was started by emancipated slaves at the end of the Civil War. The church is still in use today. Kentucky would still take four to five more days to complete, but I had enjoyed it so far.

Another cool morning had me dressing before dawn in several layers and a pair of cotton gloves. I was ready to go at first light and was surprised to see that Mathias took my advice and was almost ready to go too. He would be heading west, hoping to make San Francisco before his 90-day visa expired. We promised to stay in touch and wished each other "Safe Travels."

I rolled out with my rear light flashing. A few dogs didn't like me out that early but must not have had their nutritious breakfast yet because they lacked the energy to chase too hard. Sunrise was getting later by about 90 seconds per day, so this morning had the feel of fall. A 20-mile ride to Sonora was first up. Traffic was extremely light and most of it was through farmland again. There were no shoulders on the roads and weeds grew about five feet tall with some of them overhanging the road. I noticed that I was in another section of Amish farmland and enjoyed their well-kept farms.

It was about this time that I realized that the TransAmerica maps would take me within less than a mile of Abraham Lincoln's birthplace. The route called for me to turn east but I rode on down to the National Park to see the site. Lincoln was born in the area, but there is no historic structure to commemorate that fact. There was a slightly smaller version of the Lincoln Memorial, a nice visitor center with plenty of artifacts and much more. One of the most interesting things was the actual spring where young Abe drew water.

By this time, I was fully into the Lincoln history mode and realized that his boyhood home was less than nine miles away on the same road. I asked a park ranger about the road and she assured me that I would be fine, although one of her volunteers wasn't so sure. Regardless, I did a little planning on a Kentucky state map and found that I could easily find my way. Little did I know that later in that same day, I would have my worst mishap of the ride.

I jumped back on Highway 61 to head for Lincoln's boyhood home, all the while expecting something elaborate there, too. I easily found the site, but discovered all the buildings locked up tight. This was another example of the National Park Service cutbacks that were so prevalent in the smaller parks out west. There was a steady stream of visitors and we all walked around and gathered information as best we could. The home on the site is a replica based on drawings of what the Lincoln home looked like. Logs used to build it were taken from another home of the same time period.

One of the most interesting things that I did find out is that as a small child, Lincoln came close to drowning in a raging creek just 100 feet from the house. His best friend pulled him out with a long limb. The creek on this day was barely a trickle due to the lingering drought in the area.

As good as the Lincoln sites were so far, I was also excited to see Bardstown. As I mentioned, Stephen Foster wrote "My Old Kentucky Home" here, plus the downtown was rumored to be as historic as it was beautiful. Off I headed to Bardstown on Highway 276, still off the TransAmerica route. Everything was good so far and continued that way the last few miles into Bardstown. I climbed a huge hill into town and the target was a large distillery until I passed it and headed on into downtown. The downtown area was congested, but full of old and well-restored buildings. Once again, my cellphone wouldn't work. Verizon had poor coverage all across the TransAmerica route, but usually a decent-sized town like

Bardstown would have some service. Not this time.

My plan was to go off route again and head for Springfield and more Lincoln history. I wanted to stop and see "My Old Kentucky Home" too, and asked for directions and opinions in a very busy convenience store near the center of downtown. I was told that I could take Highway 150 to Springfield, a distance of about 17 miles. "My Old Kentucky Home" was on the way out of town on the same road. I pedaled toward the edge of town, climbing some big hills, and stopped at the "My Old Kentucky Home" State Park. Cost to see the home was $3 and cost to tour it was $7. I took the $3 deal, and found that the home was not in fact Stephen Foster's home, but that of a local judge. The home was beautiful and a nearby carillon played the state song over and over. It would have been easy to relax and enjoy the grounds, but the day was slipping away. I made photos, listened a little more and headed on toward my biggest headache of the trip.

Though the convenience store workers were sure that I would be fine on Highway 150 to Springfield, I found out quickly that there was no shoulder past the city limits and non-stop traffic in both directions. To make matters worse, rumble strips were at the edge of the road. Therefore, cyclists could not even use the edge and were more exposed to traffic. I rode about three miles out of town, hoping desperately that traffic would abate soon. Suddenly a tractor-trailer passed me while nearly clipping my handlebars. I jerked the bike over and ran over the rumble strips. The bike hit the grass on the other side and slipped out from under me, forcing my head to fall back into the road. Thankfully, the traffic stopped in both directions, all except the tractor-trailer that forced me off the road. I was bloodied pretty good, and a little shook up. I waved to the traffic to go ahead and they began to move.

The bike wasn't damaged, but I had cuts on the knee, elbow and fingers. I had banged my shoulder, hip and head, but nothing was seriously hurt. I decided to walk for a while, but even this had to be done in the grass on the side of the road. I was still at least 14 miles from Springfield and anticipated a long walk at just slightly better than 3 mph. This had become the worst afternoon of my coast-to-coast trip.

I kept walking for most of the next seven miles, then decided to experiment. I would use my mirror to see the tractor-trailers coming from behind and if any were coming from up ahead also, then I would just pull off the road and wait until they passed. During this time I realized part of the reason for the accident was my own fault. The road was narrow, narrower than many others that I had been on. By deciding to ride on such a narrow and busy road, I was putting myself and others in a bad place.

My plan worked, and I eventually got to the last three miles before Springfield. The road suddenly had huge shoulders and much less traffic. I found out later that I was then on a new section of the highway. My prayers had worked and I began to feel that I could complete the challenging ride safely. At almost 7 p.m., I rolled into Springfield, though much too late to see any historical sites. With some local help, I found the only motel and booked a room while bleeding on the counter. This had simply not been my afternoon. To make matters worse, I found out several days later when my cellphone worked again that a childhood friend, now living in Bardstown, had been following the story and wanted me to stop by. By the time I got the message, it was too late and I was more than 100 miles east.

I hit the grocery store and local Wendy's hard for massive amounts of food and settled into my room to heal and get myself back together. This had been a tough, 82-mile day. I went back to clean up my blood from the check-in counter, but the night manager had already done it. She helped me figure out a route to get to Berea, Kentucky, starting early the next morning. She assured me that I would be able to take the same Highway 150 with much greater success the next morning, and best news of all, there were shoulders all the way to Danville. I hoped she was right. It was with a touch of dread that I drifted off to sleep that night.

The next morning was cool again. I had loaded up on the continental breakfast and waited again until there was light in the sky. So far, so good. I walked my bike down the hill and headed out again on Highway 150. With little traffic and fantastic shoulders, I was feeling much better. My first town was Perryville, about 15 miles from Springfield. The shoulders ran out just as traffic started to pick up. Visions of the previous afternoon danced in my head, but I rode on through Perryville and continued on the highway. Just as I left town, I got an unexpected gift. Full shoulders returned on the road, making the increasing traffic less of a worry. Those shoulders carried me all the way to Danville, Kentucky, where bike lanes took me through town.

One interesting historical marker caught my attention. Well before modern medicine, a local doctor operated on a lady who had a huge growth in her abdomen. She remained awake throughout the surgery, singing hymns the whole time. The tumor weighed 30 pounds. She recovered and lived a normal life thereafter.

A challenging ride on Highway 52 took me to Lancaster. I felt like I was back in the Ozark Hills again with constant rolling hills and just enough traffic to keep me on edge. It was a tight little road with no shoulders. I rolled into Lancaster and asked for help with directions to Berea, Kentucky. Berea was the end of Map 10. Four people gathered around to analyze what I should do, and they all agreed. I should stay on Highway 52, then take 954 to Berea. I loaded up on food and the convenience store owner let me use the employee-only bathroom. A few more hills and I was on my way to Berea.

Imagine my surprise as Highway 52 more resembled an interstate highway on the other side of town. A wide, four-lane road with plenty of shoulder, then eventually a two lane with plenty of shoulder got me to 954 rather easily. Road 954 had some challenges with narrow and blind turns, but the traffic was mostly headed to nearby Berea and very courteous. By mid-afternoon, I was sitting in front of the Daniel Boone monument in Berea, just across from the college. I saw the huge Boone's Tavern and walked around the historic downtown briefly. I had finished Map 10.

CHAPTER 17
— Berea, Kentucky to Damascus, Virginia —

Coal trucks, bad dogs and thoughts of home

Western Kentucky differs very much from eastern Kentucky. My ride so far in the western part of the state had been nice except for the traffic issues, partly brought on by me. Tales from other cyclists about massive coal trucks and bad dogs made me a little wary of the remaining portion of Kentucky, but I was ready to take it on.

Before leaving Berea, Kentucky, I explored a bit. Daniel Boone, who purportedly lived in a cave just east of my home county, had trekked from Salisbury, North Carolina, to Berea in 1775. That journey over what is now called the Wilderness Trail opened up Kentucky for civilization and established settlements such as Boonesborough. Boone's name is all over town and a monument is dedicated to the Wilderness Trail near the oldest part of town. Berea College is also dominant in the same historical area. The college was founded in 1855 and is unique in several ways. Berea College only admits academically gifted students, primarily from the Appalachia region, and charges them no tuition. Current enrollment is about 1,500 students.

Before leaving Berea, I called ahead to a motel in McKee to check availability. The owner told me he would make sure I had a room since I was cycling across America. I stopped at the last convenience store to fill up on fluids and ice cream before heading out. The motel owner told me to expect some challenges on the 30-mile ride to McKee, especially the "Big Hill." I was determined that any hill at this point could be climbed, although I was concerned why any mountain now would be called Big Hill. I once ran a 10K in Hendersonville, North Carolina, that had an arrow on the road pointing toward their version of the big hill. Climbing that hill as a runner was hard, and I expected this one to be much the same.

The small crossroads of Big Hill came first and I headed east through a section with some Civil War history. Soon, I found the "Big Hill." As I started the climb, I realized that it was going to be steep and long. On the plus side, there were good shoulders and no traffic issues. I vowed to make the climb without pushing the bike, to see how far my climbing skills have improved. Eventually I made it to the top, which a few motorists noted with toots of their horns. A significant rock formation on both sides of the road showed just how steep the grade was, making my climbing test a huge success. There were several more climbs later, all less than the Big Hill, but with narrow roads and blind curves. Enough trucks ran on these roads to make the ride harrowing at times. Finally, after lots of climbing, I started a long gradual downhill toward McKee.

McKee was a small town with less than 500 people, but plenty of services. It had two sections of downtown, and I got directions from a police officer to find the motel. I pulled into the parking lot, and noticed that only a couple cars were there. The motel owner was close by and already had a room set aside. The WiFi didn't work in that room so he moved me to another one. It didn't work there either, but I could sit on a bench outside the room and access it. That suited me just fine. I stopped at the dairy bar twice and the grocery store once, and I was ready for a relaxing evening.

Total mileage for the trip so far was at 3,520. My plan continued to be that once I reached Damascus, Virginia, I would head south toward home. I would finalize my route in a few days.

For the first time in the whole trip, I overslept a little in McKee. The morning was overcast and foggy, so my internal clock wasn't quite as sharp. I headed uphill immediately out of McKee, something that had been hard for me since day one. My legs did not like riding uphill first thing, especially for long periods of time. The forecast called for heavy rain, and the TV said that there was lots of rain already in the area.

The first 20 miles of the morning ride gently rolled through a lightly traveled section of remote farmland. I noticed quite a few abandoned homes and farms. I wondered what stories the houses might tell if they could talk. I was getting close to the area where vicious dogs were supposed to be looking for cyclists, so I planned to stop at the first town and get ready for them. The first town was Boonville and it had a Dollar General. I started to go in and check on pepper spray. If they didn't have it, one cyclist had told me how well a water pistol loaded with ammonia worked. One well-placed shot and the dogs retreated quickly. As I quickly found out, Boonville was suffering from a power outage that morning and the Dollar General staff couldn't get in the front door. The staff and customers waited outside. I kept rolling.

Next up was Buckhorn. Not much was happening there, but I did get a few friendly waves. On to Chavies, a town where no one seemed to smile. I stopped at a convenience store and asked about WiFi. The clerk said she knew that the store had it, but she didn't know how to use it. She claimed that no one knew the password. I asked about getting ice. They had no ice in the store, but I was welcome to buy a bag outside. I bought a couple of snacks and got away before my own mood suffered. Not a vehicle was moving on the street. I did check the outside water spigot before I left. Of course, it was turned off and looked like it hadn't been used in a while. It was good to put Chavies behind me.

The terrain was tough enough that I soon realized that this was not going to be a high-mileage day. The only possible motel was in a town called Hazard, squarely in the center of coal mining country. So far, I had not seen a single coal truck because apparently they don't run on Saturdays. I saw quite a few parked beside the road. Many of them were in Chavies. The rest of the ride was uneventful. Convenience store availability had changed dramatically. Throughout most of my ride, even through western Kentucky, stores of any kind were not abundant. Convenience stores were the norm and often the center of activity in a very small town or crossroads, yet they were far apart. Suddenly, the convenience stores were much closer. No longer did I need to stop at every one.

I made it to Hazard, but was confused on how to find the motel. There seemed to be a main road and a bypass. I took the bypass and stopped at a grocery store. A worker there told me that the motel in town was about 3-4 miles away, which didn't seem right. I took his directions and found it to be just over a mile ride. Hazard also made my list of great little towns. There was lots of activity around town on Saturday evening, including stuff going on in the parks. The motel owner had some suggestions on food and groceries, and also some thoughts on directions for the next day. I headed for a sit-down evening meal and some groceries. I rode the bike and found that all of the drivers were courteous and often waved as they passed me. I had several conversations about my bike and my travels. Others went out of their way to give directions and help. Total mileage for today was 71, and I was happy with it.

One highlight of the day was a meeting with another westbound cyclist. He was from Beijing, China, and spoke in broken English. Yet, once again, a foreigner had made his first trip to the United States to ride across the country on his bike. Xiao An Zhang was friendly and seemed so happy to be here. We talked for a while about his ride. He had a late start heading west, but Xiao wasn't worried because he was taking the southern route across the desert to San Francisco. Like Mathias Erb from Berlin, they were going to avoid the early cold of the high Colorado mountains by staying south at lower elevations. Westbound cyclists were getting late if they were headed north through Wyoming, Montana, Idaho and Oregon. Cold weather would be arriving in September and some snow was possible in the highest elevations. Xiao had a unique approach to dealing with the dogs he had already encountered. He stopped, got off behind his bike and threw rocks at them. This plan had worked so far, so I began to collect a few rocks instead of worrying about pepper spray. Xiao was the last cross-country westbound cyclist that I met. We wished each other "Safe Travels" and waved goodbye.

I settled in for a contented evening in my comfortable motel room. I ate, caught up on messages, continued to eat, watched a little TV, continued to eat and submitted my story to the paper. I went to bed as a thunderstorm pounded the area. More cool weather was predicted following the storm. I went to bed hoping that another off-route adventure on Sunday would be a success. The Sunday ride should keep the coal trucks at bay for at least another day.

Sunday morning dawned cloudy, but slightly cooler. Hazard is just about three miles south of the TransAmerica Trail, but instead of going directly back to join it, I planned to take the advice of Teresa Combs from the Combs Motel and head southeast. Highway 15 was a better road to see some spectacular scenery. I would have one more day without coal trucks to make good time. Hazard is located on the north fork of the Kentucky River, and has become the center of coal mining activity. Most of the land belongs to coal companies, and thousands of tons of soft coal have been shipped from near Hazard alone. Large seams of land have been used for strip mining, a process that takes away the natural cover and exposes the soil. One report says that 70,000 men have been totally disabled from black lung disease caused by breathing coal dust long-term. I found most of the people cheerful and nice and fiercely proud of the coal mining industry. Everywhere I went, my bike and clothes seemed to generate conversations about my trip. "Where did you start?" "How far are you going?" "Will it take all summer?" These coal mining people were genuinely sincere in wanting to know about it.

Out of Hazard early, I headed down Highway 15 to Whitesburg, Kentucky. Most of the road was slightly downhill, but it kept me honest with several significant climbs. I ate a late breakfast at the McDonald's in Whitesburg, and then headed northeast on Highway 119/23 toward the town of Lookout. Just before Lookout, I stopped at a nice convenience store and ice cream shop and fueled up for a heavy climb that was just around the corner. The store was busy and several customers stopped to talk as I ate my ice cream. It was midday Sunday and the pace seemed more relaxed because of it. I rode away after having made several new friends, headed for Lookout and a big climb, which came first on narrow roads that were not well kept. There was no shoulder, and some of the pavement needed repair. The top of the mountain should have been a scenic spot, but there was so much trash around that I found it hard to see anything else. The end of the climb was steep and I had to push my bike over part of it. I was sweating like crazy. Once again, the sweat was dripping off my elbows.

Usually, I get to enjoy coasting down the other side of a mountain, but the same problems existed on the other side. There was no clear view ahead to watch for traffic and I held my speed down because of it. As I approached Lookout, I had no idea how to find the hostel that I hoped to stay in. My cellphone still wouldn't work, so I stopped to ask at yet another booming convenience store. Less than another mile on the same road was the Freida Harris Baptist Center, another cyclist's hostel. I rode on down and checked in with Greg Whitetree. The center had a gym, a clothing recycling project, and much more. For the cyclists, there was a full kitchen, a shower, free food and plenty of room. I rode back to the store and ordered a pizza and a pineapple milkshake, all the while talking with the store staff, then eventually headed back down to the Baptist center.

I had now been on the road for 49 days and over 3,600 miles. Today's mileage was 67. I still found new adventures every day, and my body had held up well. I had no real issues, only tiredness and soreness in my arms and shoulders by the end of the day. I caught up with messages and my update to the paper, then ate and showered before heading to bed early. I wanted the next day to be a big one and I hoped to say goodbye to Kentucky.

After a good night's sleep on tumbling mats on the gym floor at the Baptist Center, I woke up to a chilly morning. I had already cut the air conditioning off during the night as the temperature plunged into the low 50s. A cool morning was much appreciated on what I anticipated to be a big climbing day. Mountains surrounded me and I didn't expect to see the sun until much later in the morning. I was concerned that the coal trucks would be using the same roads as me, and I had to learn the give and take of that process.

My first town was Ashcamp after a few challenging roads. Ashcamp had some nice architecture and little traffic, so the morning was off to a good start. On the way to Elkhorn City, I got to follow a creek downhill on a fast stretch of about eight miles. Doing this brought back memories of the nice rides beside the streams in the western states. Along this road were my first serious encounters with dogs. At one time, four of them came rushing at me. Just a few kicks and a fast downhill put them in my rearview mirror while they stood disappointed in the road. Another encounter was over much quicker as I just pedaled as fast as I could and drew away quickly.

Elkhorn City was my last town in Kentucky. It must have been on the coal truck route because I saw plenty of them. Both tractor-trailers and very large dump trucks passed me regularly. If I had them coming both ways, I just got off the road and waited while they passed by. I crossed the river and began climbing regularly on some long hills. The trucks seemed to struggle as much or more than I did. I came to the Virginia line and did a little celebration fist pump. There were many good things about Kentucky, but I couldn't understand why it had rumble strips on nearly every road. Almost all of them were on the edge of the road, too, which meant that a cyclist couldn't ride that same edge. In contrast, Virginia, North Carolina and South Carolina seldom if ever had rumble strips. Maybe drivers in Kentucky had a harder time staying awake.

Historically, I saw one thing of note. Near the Virginia line, I stopped at a memorial to the Unknown Soldier of the Confederacy.

It is on a big bluff over a river at a beautiful site.

I continued climbing a series for hills called "the Breaks." When they were finally completed, I was the one who needed a break and soon stopped in Haysi at the busiest convenience store I saw on my whole journey. People were coming and going constantly in the parking lot and the same in the store. I had to lean my bike against the payphone area, nearest the road. Once again, I found the clerks polite, and they offered ice to go in my water bottles. The temperature had only climbed to 69 degrees by noon.

Other towns along the way were Birchleaf, Bee, Davenport and Council. All were either just before a mountain, just after one or both. These towns didn't believe in flat land. My next town was Honaker, where I asked directions to make sure that I had made the right turn. All seemed good, with less than 10 miles until I could call it a day.

As I headed out of town, I felt my fourth flat tire come quickly on the rear tire. I pulled into a realty office and told the lady inside that I would be outside fixing my tire. By now, I was a little more organized at doing the repair than I had been out west. I had all my tools and tubes in the same pannier, and had a pair of gloves to wear just for this purpose. Changing the tube on a rear tire can be messy, so the gloves came in handy. Off came the tire after unhooking the brakes and getting the tire past the chain. Out came the damaged tube that had a hole the size of a dime. Back in went a new one, and back on went the tire, chain and brakes. I started to pump up the tire, and a local resident named Benny Martin stopped in to help. Benny offered to take me and the bike somewhere to get the tire pumped up enough to ride, but I then remembered the CO_2 cartridge remaining in my bag. I pulled it out, and pumped the tire up to specs quickly. Benny was impressed. I told him where I was headed to spend the night and asked him to call ahead and tell them that I was on the way. Benny did just that. I thanked Benny and headed on out while promising to call once I reached my overnight accommodations.

Benny could easily have left it at that, but he didn't. I rode on to Rosedale over a challenging hill that Benny warned me about. In Rosedale, I asked the location of the Elk Garden Methodist Church that offers a hostel for cyclists. I got three different answers and none of them were exactly right. My best move of the night was to go ahead and load up on food at the convenience store before heading out to find the church. While waiting on an order of crazy bread, I talked farming with a local resident. We discussed how much rain had fallen in both Virginia and North Carolina during the spring and summer. This farmer had not been able to cut his spring hay and was worried about when he might be able to cut.

On I went to find the church with an order of crazy bread hanging out of my pannier. I didn't see it and was well past where at least two of the directions led me. I pulled off the road, checked my phone and once again found no service. Just at that time, the nearest home owner pulled in and I asked her where the church was. She told me to turn left at the next intersection and I would see it. For some reason, it didn't surprise me that she was absolutely right. I was now late and was afraid that no one would be around to let me in the church. There was not anyone there when I did find the church, but I found the door unlocked and a sign welcomed me in. Inside was everything I needed, including a kitchen, food in the refrigerator and outside was plenty of room to park the bike underneath a big shelter outside. I put my stuff inside and headed for the bike to store it for the night. I wanted to check out the outside shower on an already cool evening too. Quickly, I spotted the outside shower and saw a water hose hooked to it. I realized that being tough enough to ride across the country didn't mean that I was tough enough to take a 50-degree shower on cool evening.

I was ready to head back inside and noticed a car pulling up in the driveway. It was Benny Martin, the man who stopped to help me in Honaker. He brought his girlfriend and introduced her, but he also brought me six CO2 cartridges. Benny had also bought some for himself and planned to use one when he had to fix the next flat on his own bike. We talked about his family, and the rest of my ride, then promised to keep in touch. Good people like Benny made my trip so enjoyable.

After Benny left, I considered the shower again. No doubt that I needed one, but just couldn't make myself face the cold. It was time for food and the usual nighttime work on my iPad. There was no WiFi, so my replies and newspaper update would have to wait until morning. I put my sleeping bag and air mattress on a big plastic table and went to bed early, once again comfortable in a church environment. All in all, I think my best nights of sleep came in the churches along the way.

One humorous note from the day's ride included climbing a mountain called the Big A Mountain. That probably trumped climbing the "Big Hill" just a couple of days ago.

Once again, I was up early with a plan for the day. My goal was to make it to Damascus, Virginia, and get the bike checked out. The lower gears were just too noisy and I knew something needed work. I read that Damascus had some good hostels, so I considered spending an afternoon there. Also, it would be great if I could get some advice on the best way over the mountains and back to Rowan County and home.

My next goal was to climb Webb Mountain after cycling a few miles through an agricultural area. This was a cool morning, and traffic was almost non-existent. Over my whole journey, I don't think I enjoyed another mountain as much. The trees formed a green canopy over the road and the only sounds were made by my bike. Best yet, I climbed the less steep side of the mountain and the other side gave me a nice coasting ride to the bottom. I stopped in Hayter's Gap to transmit my messages, but found the library closed until 11 a.m., so I kept on rolling.

The Virginia countryside was absolutely beautiful, with another round of old homes and beautiful farms. I even saw a herd of cows with bells tied around their necks. There was no trash along the roads, a big change from what I had seen in eastern Kentucky. This was a nice morning for a bicycle ride.

Next town was Meadowview, home of another busy convenience store. My bags were quickly filled with energy foods, and with less than 15 miles to Damascus, I headed off on more scenic roads and climbed a few hills in anticipation of an early afternoon off.

Damascus is a center of activity for the Virginia Creeper Trail, as well as the TransAmerica Trail and Appalachian Trail. Cyclists and hikers, as well as tourists in general, are everywhere. Several bike shops were listed, but I didn't know anything about them. I pulled into town and immediately asked help from a local who was picking up trash along the Creeper Trail. Bill explained the differences in the bike shops in town, and then eventually led me to the one that he recommended. Bill said that Gary was the best bike mechanic in town, and that we should see if he was available. We found Gary and Bill explained to him that I needed some maintenance on the bike. Gary immediately went to work on the bike and found that grit had accumulated between the gear teeth. He used a piece of cardboard to clean most of it out, then went about oiling the chain as he shifted through all the gears. Gary finished the bike and didn't charge me a thing. The bike was ready for more riding, so I headed for Subway to have lunch and use their WiFi, and decide about the rest of the day.

CHAPTER 18
— Damascus, Virginia to Rowan County, NC —

A tough but very rewarding journey home

I had to make a big decision. I had half a day left and could either rest in Damascus for the afternoon, gather information for the best route home, and get some rest for several serious climbs, or I could push on and fly by the seat of my pants. My body was worn down after 50 consecutive days of pedaling. An afternoon of rest might make it easier for the final journey toward home.

I scanned the remaining part of the TransAmerica Map 11 and studied several routes on MapQuest with my iPad. I knew from talking with Bill and Gary in Damascus that I would face a serious climb toward Mount Rogers soon after I left Damascus. There would also be more tough climbs on the way to North Carolina, including Whitetop Mountain and the ascent to the Grayson Highlands.

By shortly after 1 p.m., I made my decision to keep going and make the best I could of the rest of the day. I had no real expectations of where I might end up. But with no second guessing, I headed home and would do my best to get a significant portion of it completed that afternoon.

I had Subway cookies, and some more food loaded in my bags and was well aware that food stops through the Whitetop Mountain and Grayson Highlands areas would be limited. These would be my last major climbs on my coast-to-coast journey.

My map suggested that I could use the Virginia Creeper Trail for part of the journey. I rode about a mile on it, then found a path through the woods back to the road. My bike was just not suitable to ride over the rocks and sometimes rough terrain of the Creeper

Trail, nor did I like the idea of being in the middle of all the tourist bicycle traffic headed back to Damascus from Whitetop.

Back on the road, I knew the climb would be much worse. I stayed on the TransAmerica Trail until just before the crossroads of Konnarock. The first eight miles were challenging and then the climb leveled out for a while. When Highway 58 left the trail and turned southeast, I knew that I was headed for home. It was a landmark moment and I stopped long enough to take a photo of that sign. There was significant climbing to do right away as the road continued up past Whitetop Mountain. Once again, traffic was light and I was thankful for that. The roads were narrow and it was a cloudy and gloomy afternoon. Still, I felt energized because I had no idea how far I could make it on that day or where I might spend the night.

My route continued on Highway 58, also known as the Jeb Stuart Highway. Gary had made my gears and shifters work better than they had in weeks, and the bike was quieter overall than I remembered when it was new. I stopped to snack a few times along the way, but kept climbing on up past the Grayson Highlands. In the back of my mind, I knew that there would still be small climbs as I headed home, but I had completed the last big climb.

I kept seeing signs for Mouth of Wilson, Virginia, and thought that I could get there before dark. I didn't know anything about Mouth of Wilson, except that Oak Hill Academy is there. Oak Hill is known for fine prep basketball teams, so I thought there would be at least a town. I pushed on through the 12 miles from Grayson Highlands to Mouth of Wilson, most of it downhill. I passed Oak Hill Academy and then looked for the town. There was none. I even looped around and came back to make sure I didn't miss something. Not a store was in sight.

The North Carolina state line was close by and it was getting dark quickly. I continued on and crossed the state line less than 10 minutes later on N.C. 93. It was sure good to see that sign, although

I wondered how clear the photo would be in the advancing darkness. Another sign advertised a restaurant just a few miles away. With a little luck, there would be someone at the restaurant who could suggest a place to camp. Quickly, I found the restaurant and the sign that said it was only open on Thursday through Sunday, and again there was no one around. Nothing to do but keep pedaling. I saw a resident in his yard and asked him about a motel or campground. He said that the nearest motel was in Sparta, more than 20 miles away. There was, however, a campground about 10 miles away, but he wasn't sure if it was still open. It was about five miles off N.C. 93. No way was I going to chase it, so I rode on in hopes of finding a convenience store that the resident also mentioned. With dark closing in under an overcast sky, I pulled into Maria Hurtado's convenience store and told her my dilemma. She quickly offered me a spot to camp behind the store, and she had an outside bathroom. Maria was my angel of the night as she quickly made me some food on her grill before closing time. Maria also left me a note for the sheriff's deputies should they question why I was camping behind the store. Just before dark, I pitched my tent and had a nice meal of grilled cheese sandwiches, potato chips, Reese's Cups and ice cream. I composed my story on the day's happenings and expected a good night's sleep after 77 total miles.

During the night, a light rain began to fall, as predicted. Over the length of my whole trip, I had gradually grown to like camping. The first few nights were disasters, largely because I bought a cheap tent based on weight. Once I had a good one, I had no worries about setup or leaking. On this night, sleep came so easily and I didn't toss and turn. The sound of the rain drops just added to the peacefulness of the night. I did wake up several times and wondered if it would be possible to push all the way home in one more day.

Up early the next morning, I stood under the overhang to pack my gear and keep it dry at the same time. There was no traffic again, so I set out in the rain hoping to find my way from memory and a few notes since there was still no cellphone or WiFi coverage to use my iPad. My first turn was a left on to Highway 221, but I didn't remember how far it was. Once I found that turn, I could get really excited about the day. The rain increased in intensity and I worried that I somehow had missed the turn, but then celebrated greatly at the sight of it. A long and gently rolling road carried me past neat yards and large Christmas tree farms. Some of the farms were up on small mountains on my right and left as it seemed that I was riding through a valley. For the most part, I had the road to myself. Highway 221 led to Sparta, and I stopped at a little market and confirmed that my directions were good. The owner just couldn't believe that anyone would ride a bike so far.

By this time, I was still not sure how far I could go. I felt strong, but the climbing was still significant enough that I was only averaging about nine miles an hour. Sparta had several climbs coming into the town, but eventually I rode down Main Street until I saw a coffee shop. They always have good WiFi, so I pulled up in front of the shop, stayed on my bike and transmitted my story and replied to messages from the previous day. I headed out of Sparta into some more climbing and no shoulders on the road. There was just enough traffic to keep me on my toes.

In Roaring Gap, I noticed that the hills were shrinking. My pace was improving, and continued to do so on south to Jonesville where suddenly Highway 21 South Bypass placed me on Interstate 77. After legally riding on the interstate highways in three states, I wondered if those experiences would aid my explanation should I get stopped by the North Carolina Highway Patrol. At the next exit in Jonesville, I quickly left the interstate and asked for directions as to how to get around this situation. Two clerks at the first gas station didn't know how, but a customer told me that his friend outside would know how to do it. Then the customer said, "Wait a minute, I know who you are! You are the guy who is riding across the country. My daughter has followed it all." He took my picture and passed me off to his friend for directions. Those directions were perfect and about three miles later I was headed south again on the right road.

I kept rolling and logged 50 miles by noon. As expected, the hills had continued to decline. I was sure that if all went well, 100 miles by late in the afternoon was possible. I was going to make it home that night! Tears welled in my eyes. This was the first emotional moment for the end of the trip, but it wouldn't be my last. The rain still fell, but the skies were slowly improving. A break in the rain would help, but wasn't critical.

Just north of Harmony, the highway again became hilly. I pulled into a store and ate my last ice cream of the day there, and verified that I was about 20 miles north of Statesville. I called one of my daughters and told her that I would make it home that night, hopefully by 7 p.m.

Past Harmony, the next town was Turnersburg. Rain had started to fall again. By the time I reached Statesville, the rain was a heavy downpour and flooding had started. I knew how to get home in a car, but hoped that a local could tell me the shortest way on my bike. After much discussion in a convenience store, I had directions that seemed good. The last climb of the day was up through the downtown area of Statesville. I missed the turn and had to ask again. By rush hour, I was in a heavy downpour on a four-lane Highway 70 and headed home.

Drivers gave me plenty of room, probably thinking that only a crazy fool would ever want to ride a bike in such weather. Little did they know that I was headed home from western Oregon. At this point, I had less than 20 miles left, and I was confident of making it. I turned off of Highway 70 on to Highway 801, and then White Road. Although I didn't believe it could, the rain poured down even harder and a strong wind pushed me backward. I pulled into Mt. Zion Baptist Church and took shelter under an overhang for a few minutes. I had no food or drink for about 30 miles, so this was a good time to have some cookies and water. It almost felt like a celebratory meal. Eventually the rain let up slightly and the wind died down. I had to go. I was about three miles from home.

I turned on Lyerly Road, then Kerr Mill, then Sloan, and then Millbridge. Just one more turn left. I turned on Weaver Road, and once again a small amount of tears came. I saw my farm and realized that I had made it home, all the way from Oregon. Today's ride was 110 miles.

There would be no real celebrating yet. I had to ride another 200 miles to reach the Atlantic Ocean. With good fortune and more prayers, two more days of riding would complete my grand journey.

CHAPTER 19
— Rowan County, NC to Myrtle Beach, SC —

The home stretch, with traffic challenges and lots of anticipation

I spent two days at home, getting myself together for the final ride to the Atlantic Ocean. My bike was in good shape, and I felt strong. I decided to ride to Myrtle Beach, the closest of all the beaches.

Based on my recent daily mileages and the fact that there would not be any major hills on this ride, the ride should last only two days. Total mileage between home and Myrtle Beach was about 200 miles, and Bennettsville, South Carolina, was near the halfway point. I knew what I had to do, and couldn't wait to get after it. But this portion of the ride was going to have some high traffic areas, especially the last 60 miles to the beach. My plan was to leave early on Saturday morning and push hard to Bennettsville, hoping to avoid the workday traffic. The trucks especially worried me because most of the roads on this segment don't have shoulders.

I used Thursday and Friday for planning and preparation. I took the panniers off the bike and emptied them. I wanted my bags efficiently packed with less things and a lower total weight. I had less need for large amounts of food and water. The tent and sleeping bag would stay home. I packed a few beach clothes, too.

I washed my riding clothes, including my lucky shirt and socks. I even washed my shoes. The bright yellow shirt had kept me visible for 52 riding days, and it was good for two more.

I checked the bike, and even called the local bike shop. In my absence, Skinny Wheels Bike Shop had started to set up a new shop in Salisbury. It wasn't open yet though, so I decided that the tires, tubes and chain could easily last for two more hard days.

I got a haircut on Thursday afternoon. Many folks advised me to rest. They just didn't understand. I would rest when the trip was complete. My first night in my own bed after nearly two months didn't go well. I was restless and kept dreaming that I needed to be riding. On Friday, I did some yard work and visited with the horses. They all got their manes trimmed and a few tangles worked out. I was glad that they remembered me. I mowed most of the yard and sprayed some weed killer. Later, I watched a ball game, ate a lot and then went to bed. It was time to get the final show on the road.

There was light in the sky and a break in some low-lying fog about 6:30 a.m. It felt good to be back on the bike, especially hauling less weight. My pace was good as I rode the rural roads to Rockwell and my planned intersection with Highway 52 South. Pam Roseman, one of our local Ironman triathletes, was waiting for me beside the road. It was a delight to see her and get yet another fantastic wish for good luck and safety on the ride. Highway 52 is normally busy on a weekday, but my choice of a Saturday departure seemed perfect. Traffic remained light, even after the road turned into a four-lane at Richfield. I noticed that my front tire was just a tad down on air, so I stopped in Albemarle to take care of it.

My first stop was a used-car lot, where the salesman told me that the only free air in town was at a convenience store just a block away. I backtracked, got the air and bought some food. My discussion with the used car salesman had centered on whether air should be free. I told him that out West, convenience stores and markets seldom charged for air. Just as they are important to the towns of less than 100 people, their prices are not out of line even though the nearest alternative might be 50 miles away. Thank God for convenience stores on my trip. I got food, a short rest, directions, water, ice and pleasant conversation at nearly every one of them.

Norwood was the next town, and rising temperatures had reminded me that ice cream was appropriate for lunch. I had completed 50 miles, hoping that I was halfway to my overnight stop in Bennettsville. Highway 52 had returned to a two-lane road, but still traffic was reasonable. A series of rolling hills made the road to Wadesboro more challenging, but nothing that was going to slow me down for long.

Wadesboro was the biggest town remaining on my route for that Saturday. Based on an earlier conversation, having a McDonald's made Wadesboro a real town. I pulled in to get some cookies, fries and use the WiFi. Just as I was about to leave, Derek Freeze from China Grove and his fiancée, Julie, stopped by my table. They had followed the story of the ride and were on the way to the beach, too. It was good to see them and this was yet another boost to my day.

I left Wadesboro with an estimated 36 more miles to go for the day with the first significant town being Cheraw. My water bottles had ice and I was ready for the more challenging segment to Cheraw. Several long hills were only mere obstacles on this day. My climbing had improved so much that I had little trouble with them.

It was good to see the South Carolina sign, knowing that this would be the last state on my journey. I also knew that the road would be flat or slightly downhill for most of the remaining ride. I made the last state sign picture and headed on to Cheraw, thinking of ice cream yet again.

A sheriff's deputy rode by me a couple of times, and then after a few minutes stopped beside me on the road with his lights all flashing. The deputy said, "Sir, this is a busy road and people might not be looking for you. Be real careful on your ride today." This was the first time in now close to 4,100 miles that a law enforcement officer had pulled over to tell me to be careful. Maybe I took the statement a little harshly as I pedaled in sync with his car speed. My answer was, "I am being careful! I just rode here from Oregon." Immediately he cut the lights off and drove away, probably thinking that this guy was a crackpot or maybe that he really had ridden that far.

Either way, he left me alone the rest of the afternoon.

I was thrilled to see Cheraw and the turn to the beach. I came to the intersection of Highway 52 and Highway 9, and quickly spotted Baskin Kreme Kastle. They made me the best pineapple milkshake and gave me some ice water, too. My only request was, "This ice cream needs to get me 20 more miles." Nobody could believe that I was riding to the beach, much less from Oregon. I vowed to stop in again as I drove home in a few days.

The last miles to Bennettsville were pleasant, with plenty of road room and cooling temperatures. It was peaceful knowing that my next to last day was coming to an end and it had gone well. I pulled into Bennettsville and headed straight for the Marlboro Inn. It didn't have the best reputation, but recent reviews sounded OK. My first clue was the manager kept his door locked. My second was that the WiFi wouldn't connect and my third was that the ice machine looked like it hadn't been used in the last five years. I looked at a room and quietly made another call to the Williams Motel. I wasn't going to spend my last night on the road in a less than reasonable room, especially after so many other great experiences throughout the country. The Williams Motel was clean, the owner responsive, had the biggest ice machine yet and ended up being my home for the night after 110 miles completed. I got a good night's sleep. One more day to go.

August 4, 2013, the last planned day of my ride. With a little sadness, I mounted the bike for a short ride to McDonald's and a light breakfast. It was easy to enjoy this life of a nomad, avoiding the real life back home, complete with bills and time demands and responsibilities. I was excited to get to the beach and see the Atlantic, just 56 days after I left the Pacific Ocean behind in Oregon.

I knew the route by heart to Myrtle Beach, so I needed no map. Up and out at 6 a.m., I wanted to get ahead of the inbound beach traffic. Highway 38 from Bennettsville was four-lane, with occasional shoulders. It looks smooth in a car, but it's rough on a bike.

I weaved back and forth in my lane, hoping to find the smoothest spots. Traffic was still light and the first 25 miles went by quickly.

The final turn on to Highway 501 meant that traffic would be heavy the rest of the way, more than 60 miles. Four lanes of highway were thick with traffic, which wouldn't have been a problem except for the return of the dreaded rumble strips. Was it possible that somebody from Kentucky had built this road in South Carolina? There was virtually no shoulder and the rumble strips ran right up to the white line. I had no choice but to voice my motto yet again, "Ride with me, Lord," as the traffic continued to build.

About this time, Bradley Eagle, a friend from home, pulled up beside me on his motorcycle. Bradley was riding to the beach to see my wheel dipping, so he then pulled off just ahead of where we had talked. Bradley offered to get me water and circle back around, and seemed genuinely worried about the amount of traffic. We made plans to meet later that afternoon. Back into the traffic I went.

I made sure to watch in my helmet mirror as much as I could what was happening behind me. Still with only a few trucks on the road, the cars gave me room and were courteous. I watched them maneuver to ease over behind me. My confidence in them grew as I passed Aynor and headed to Conway. This city stretches out for several miles and has lots of traffic lights, so the pace of the traffic was slowed quite a bit. The temperature was nearing 90 degrees, but didn't seem so bad. There were even a few shoulders on occasion. Just 20 miles remained in my coast-to-coast ride. In that odd moment, I shed just a few small tears.

I left Conway knowing that traffic would remain somewhat subdued because of a long series of lights. I made up some time as the long lines of cars had to stop often. Occasionally, a passenger in a car would roll down his window and ask about my ride. All that remained was to cover the last few miles safely. Third Avenue was just ahead and I was ready for my first sight of the ocean. Just before that, I stopped for an ice cream sandwich. The stop wasn't only to refuel, but more so to reflect on what was about to happen. My ride across America was soon to be completed successfully and I wanted to savor the moment.

Just a few minutes later, I saw the ocean and tears flowed. I had done it. The biggest adventure of my life!

I rode on to David's Landing, an appropriate name for my motel. Bradley had checked in and told them that I was going to be along soon. The motel doesn't usually allow bikes in the room, but they already had planned an exception for me. I went to my room and tried to get my thoughts together. I called Bradley and also another friend, Norma Honeycutt, to tell them that I planned the official wheel dipping for 4 p.m. My daughter, Amber, had been delayed by work and wouldn't get to the beach until the next day.

The official end was in sight.

I showered and headed down to the parking lot to meet Bradley, Norma and her husband, Mark. They shot videos and photographs that I will treasure forever. Norma filmed the video and Bradley took photos as I carried the bike down to the beach. The Atlantic Ocean is much closer than the Pacific, making the walk to the beach easier. I went barefoot because I knew I'd get my feet wet. I dipped my wheel, but kept my emotions in check. We actually ran through it a couple of times to make sure we had it all on film. Mission accomplished. The ride was complete.

It had been a great day, with the ride consisting of 88 miles. We celebrated with a nice meal and I headed back to the room for some rest.

CHAPTER 20
— My Equipment —

What worked and what didn't

As I mentioned earlier, I followed suggestions from Andrew Sufficool and other online reports about how to make my equipment list and what specific brands might work best. I wanted durability, light weight and versatile choices — items that could serve more than one purpose. Along the way, I learned some things and made a few changes and additions. At least once, I found the nearest trash can for a product that seemed fine when I started. I will explain why I chose the item, how it worked out and whether I will take it again on another long ride.

First and foremost was a quality bike. Before the trip, I didn't own a touring bike. Touring bikes differ from other road bikes in that they are built heavier, stronger and have the ability to carry extra weight. The gears, crank, frame and just about every part are ready for the long haul and heavy usage. I chose a 2013 Surly Long Haul Trucker. I estimated that about 40 percent of the bikes I encountered were Surlys. I found no one unhappy with them. My bike covered the 4,164 miles without a significant problem. I never had a broken spoke, although Surly actually mounts a couple of replacements on the frame of the bike at purchase. The only problem that I experienced was with chattering lower gears. Gary, the bike mechanic in Damascus, Virginia, told me that grit had been collecting among the rear gears for the whole trip. He took 15 minutes to clean them with a piece of stiff cardboard, and that, combined with several good chain oilings, was the extent of bike maintenance. No chain adjustments were needed.

I replaced the Surly stock seat with a Brooks B-17 saddle. The Brooks had great reviews online, although it arrived as hard as I can imagine a bike seat ever being. Most online reports said that after 500 miles the seat would conform to my butt bones. I heard lots of stories about how a mismatched bike seat made for a miserable ride. The B-17 seat is not cheap, but it's well worth the money. I spent an average of 8-10 hours a day on that seat, and never had a saddle sore. Most of the first two weeks, I used a sports lubricant to ease the friction, but soon found that I didn't need it. I highly endorse the Surly bike and the Brooks B-17 seat.

Next up were the tires and tubes. I spent two years reading about cross-country trips on "Crazy Guy on a Bike" and other websites. Problems with tires and tubes could cause a good day to go bad on a moment's notice. I chose top-of-the-line Continental Tires. They were rated for 4,000 miles. They now have close to 4,800 and still look good for at least another 1,000. I bought the best available tubes as well. I only had four flats over 4,164 miles. Three were on the rear tire and one was on the front. I found no foreign object in the tires after any of the flats. I did not patch the tubes, because I heard many stories of a tube being patched and working fine for a few days, then going flat again. Tubes are relatively inexpensive, so I immediately replaced any leaking tube with a new one.

I took the extra step of using tube liners. Placed between the tube and the tire, they are the first defense against metal, thorns or anything else that might have caused the tube to puncture.

I used a Toba rear rack on which to mount my panniers. I only carried two panniers, so I did not need a front rack, even though the Surly would have easily carried one. The rack was solid and sturdy, and it bolted to the frame in four places.

I also felt that the bike needed fenders. I knew that I would be riding in the rain often, and wanted to stay as dry from underneath as possible. My fenders were made by Planet Bike. They were light, yet functional.

I mounted two water bottle carriers, large enough for 32-ounce bottles. I saw bikes with as many as four mounted, but I just carried my extras in the panniers. Water mounted on the frame tended to get warm quickly, and those inside the bags held their temperature much longer.

This ends the portion of equipment that was permanently mounted on the bike. Other cyclists carried much more; however, my motto was "if you mount it, you have to carry it up the hills."

The next section includes items mounted in a less permanent manner.

I chose top-of-the-line Ortlieb panniers in red. Panniers are another name for saddlebags. I saw some in yellow, which would have been a good color, too. My panniers had a reflective triangle on the side of the bag, making them easily seen from the rear by other vehicles. These Ortlieb panniers were also waterproof and durable. Not a single item ever was damaged by weather or being bumped from the outside.

I later added a Trek waterproof handlebar bag. I started out carrying my "might need it quick" stuff in a backpack. That worked well for a while, but with so much handling, even a top-quality backpack was soon showing wear. Warmer temperatures caused me to heat up quickly underneath the backpack. The backpack also was not waterproof and heavy rains could get some of the material inside wet. I had spotted several cyclists using the handlebar bag, and I was intrigued by it. There were side pockets all the way around and a big open area in the middle, although the bag was only a foot wide and about eight inches deep. It bolted securely to the handlebar holder. The bag was expensive but well worth it. I kept my wallet, iPad mini, phone, change, snacks and even a soft drink in it. The Trek bag has a snap-on map case that sits on top of the bag, but I found it lacking and didn't use it. There was nothing to keep the maps from falling out the sides, particularly in the case of a good wind.

I carried a good map case that allowed for mounting two maps, one on top and one underneath the top cover. It was easy to open after choosing the portion of the map that the cyclist needed to see. It was sturdy, weatherproof and solidly velcroed to the handlebars. I continued to use it even after buying the Trek handlebar bag.

Another item that proved its worth often was a rear flashing safety light. It was plasti-tied to the pannier rack. It had a flashing choice as well as a pattern choice, and was battery operated. I did not need to change the battery once during my trip. These lights show up well in low light or fog.

I did not use a headlight. I had no intention of riding in the dark with the long summer days at hand, and most good headlights are expensive and weigh more than I wanted to carry for just emergency usage.

Still another battery-powered item was the Sigma 1009 cyclometer. This device was calibrated to the size of the front wheel and measured overall trip distance, daily distance, speed and several more things that I didn't use.

My tire pump was a mini-model MP-3 made by Serfas. The pump is about nine inches long, has its own air gauge and works on two sizes of tire valves. The pump was mounted below the water bottle holder on the frame underneath the seat by Velcro. I chose the mini-pump because of the ease of carrying. One big drawback was that it would only inflate tires to about 65 psi. This worked fine until I could get to a larger air source to further inflate the tire to 85-90 psi. CO_2 cartridges were perfect to inflate the tires also.

One item that I carried along was a high quality combination bike lock made by Krytonite. The bike shop mechanic in Astoria convinced me that thieves could target my bike, so I bought it. Weight of the lock is almost three pounds. I don't plan to carry it on the next ride.

This concludes those items that were fastened by plastic ties or Velcro to the frame.

Other items were either bungeed to the frame or carried in the panniers or handlebar bag. Most of these items are based on personal choice or availability.

My sleeping bag was a Kelty 35-degree, standard model bag, and I was totally happy with it. I spent several nights in areas with nighttime lows of 40 degrees. The bag was comfortable with only lightweight clothing worn underneath. It was kept in a waterproof bag that served as a "stuff bag" at night. I took all the remaining clothes and put them in the "stuff bag" and made a usable pillow. I heard from others that the mummy-style bags were too hot. I did not camp on the extremely hot nights, but would have probably just used the bag to lie on top of in that case. The bag worked well when I slept on picnic tables as it provided significant cushion.

My air mattress was a lightweight one made by Therma-Rest. The mattress was only long enough to extend from below my rear to slightly above my head. I never missed a longer or more inflated mattress. This mattress was easy enough to blow up with my own air. The only drawback was that this mattress stuck together if the air temperature was hot.

One of my best purchases was my new tent. I got it at an outfitter in West Yellowstone. My original tent was lightweight, but it leaked and took extra time to assemble and pack up. I trashed it in West Yellowstone and replaced it with a Skyledge tent that could sleep two people if they knew each other well. Best was the fact that this tent didn't leak and it packed up easily. I could set it up and break it down in three to five minutes each. Total weight was about 4.5 pounds.

A few items were stars of my trip, items that completely fulfilled the purpose for which they were purchased.

One of these was my tool kit. I had several items made by Bell that were especially dependable. There was a set of Allen wrenches and two plastic tire tools (used for breaking the tire loose from the rim and getting the tubes out). I also carried a spoke wrench but didn't know how to use it. After talking with a bike mechanic who told me that spoke replacement and adjustment could really be messed up by amateurs, I was glad that I didn't need it. One cyclist of about my same body size had already replaced 9 spokes and was still 1,000 miles from the coast. The mechanic told me that he probably had improperly adjusted the spokes and that was causing more breakage. I kept CO_2 cartridges in that tool kit, too, and am still amazed at how well they worked.

My rain jacket was made of Tyvek, a lightweight and durable waterproof material. Mine was yellow, and especially handy to help motorists see me. The hood worked just fine on a pullover-style jacket. The only drawback was that the jacket did not have pockets, which would have come in handy. I bought this one from Amazon and also purchased the matching pants. I never wore the pants, but would have if the conditions had been wet and slightly colder.

I carried two pairs of gloves. One was a pair of leather Nike cycling gloves with the fingers cut out. These were comfortable in all temperatures, but I did wear a pair of cotton gloves when the temperatures dropped below 50 degrees. After changing the rear tire once, I carried a pair of cotton gloves to wear when doing this again. Grease off the chain and grit off the frame and tires were easy to smear on clothes that had to be packed and unpacked as part of the process.

My Louie Garneau helmet had plenty of cushioning and was adjustable. Attached to the helmet was a rear-view mirror. Several cyclists told me that they didn't use one, but I found the mirror a must-have. I bought the top-of-the-line adjustable model in Astoria right before I left the bike shop. It was great to have a wide field of vision behind me, especially in those high-traffic situations. The helmet hit the road hard once — with my head inside — and proved its worth. My best method of wearing a hooded rain coat was to put the hood under the helmet and adjust the tightness. Some cyclists put the hood over the helmet, but I found that wind was a constant issue when done this way.

Cooking on the road was not something that I wanted to do, so

I carried no cooking apparatus or fuel. This helped me to keep my pannier total weight much lower.

Most clothing choices will be made by personal preference, but here's what worked for me. I took along a wool-blend, long-sleeved shirt that came in handy time and again in the cool weather of the Pacific and higher elevations. This shirt kept me warm and dried out easily. I also loved the wool cycling socks that I wore on the ride, especially until the hot temperatures of the plains. The socks served the same purpose as the wool shirt. Warm and dry socks were valued often. For some of the early cold and wet rides, I wore a pair of dri-fit mittens. They kept my fingers toasty when the rest of my body was freezing. I also bought a pair of insulated gloves that served the same purpose but had limited use in the rain.

I wore my cycling shorts every day. I started with a pair of Adidas shorts and wore them every single day of the ride. As a friend suggested, I showered with them every night that I could. I did the same with my dri-fit short sleeve shirt. Washing them with shampoo kept them clean and smelling nice. Both showed some wear at the end of the trip but certainly served their purpose.

A big decision that long-distance cyclists have to make is whether to wear clip-in shoes or something else. I chose Brooks running shoes — the only pair of shoes I took — because they are comfortable and I could move my feet around on the pedals and inside the cage.

Counting personal items, such as three pairs of underwear, a long-sleeved and short-sleeved shirt, extra socks, hygiene items, and a few odds and ends, I had usually had plenty of room left in my panniers for food and water. I had duct tape and a small flashlight, and usually a couple of spare tubes, but not much more. After I left the Colorado mountains, I shipped some cold-weather clothing home and that opened up even more room. Total weight of my loaded panniers, and the tent and sleeping bag, came to about 30 pounds before food and water. On average, I carried less than

40 pounds. This was much less than a lot of cyclists who appeared loaded worse than a gold rush pack horse.

After a few days on the road, I seldom felt the need for something that I didn't have.

CHAPTER 21
—A look back on my great adventure

Just over a month ago, I finished my ride and dipped the front wheel in the Atlantic Ocean at Myrtle Beach. My life has been a whirlwind since. The biggest challenge has been getting back into a more normal routine and catching up on my daily responsibilities. I'm not rushing the return to normal; in fact, I hope to delay it as long as possible.

I am having a great time in the aftermath of the ride. On one hand, I am not sure I deserve this moment in the sun. However, I have enjoyed meeting so many new people who followed the great adventure. One of my lifetime goals is to meet at least one new person each day and I am certainly exceeding that goal recently.

When I began to firm up my travel plans, the staff at our hometown newspaper agreed that it was a good idea to allow me to journal my thoughts and share them with readers. We didn't know in the beginning exactly how it would work. In fact, I thought the lifestyles editor, who had taken a real interest from our first discussions, would cover the trip. After just a few days on the road, we made the decision to cover the trip in news. That suited me and I told the newspaper staff that I would endeavor to send in daily reports, based on connectivity. I knew there would be many areas without WiFi or cellphone coverage.

I felt that a certain group that might avidly follow the adventure would include a few runners, cyclists and acquaintances. For weeks, I didn't expect anything else. As the trip progressed, I began to realize that more than a few others were following along on a daily basis. I got their e-mails of support and I loved them. Many of them offered needed prayers and I cherished every one. At least one of the close calls was too close. An encounter with a tractor-trailer nearly turned into a serious accident. I uttered, "Lord, ride with me" many times.

I started the trip with a huge anticipation and a small amount of concern whether I could do this. Each day, I gained confidence in my ability to keep going and complete the journey. The first day was probably the only time that I had serious concern as to whether I could complete a coast-to-coast ride. The first hill in Astoria was short but brutal, and I struggled to make it to the top. The reward at the top was a beautiful view of the Columbia River and the Pacific Ocean. This would be a pattern that would play out time and time again over the first week. I had no idea that the hills would be so challenging along the West Coast. Over time, my legs grew accustomed to the climbing and made much bigger and steeper climbs.

The first segment along the Pacific was just a warm up for what would come later. There was no tough traffic and the hills were not that bad. I learned how to plan my day and use the maps as they were intended. The cool and sometimes windy rain was nothing compared to the weather extremes that I would see later. Turning inland in central and eastern Oregon gave me insight into what the rest of the trip might hold. On one of these days, I called a friend back home and told her, "I am sure I can do this. Today was a magical day!" And so it went for many more days.

My days fell into a specific pattern. I would rise as early as possible on most days, and be on the road before sunrise. Full days ended at 4-6 p.m. usually, but on occasion they continued to 7 or 8 p.m. As the ride developed, I wouldn't accept less than 60 miles per day, had a minimum goal of at least 70 miles, and hoped for more. I never was tired enough that a light afternoon coupled with a little extra downtime wouldn't fix. My day was totally about the ride. I handled communications from home at night.

I loved the sunrises and long flat stretches. But the part of the day that I loved the most was the late afternoon and evening. With the day's ride done and acceptable total mileage completed for the day, I was able to relax and eat off and on for several hours. It was the only part of the day that I could spend any real time planning and I took advantage of it. I spread out my current TransAmerica map and a state map and then analyzed the best way to proceed the next day. This was the best time to call for motel rates in my projected next destination. If I thought that cell service might be sporadic, I might even call for the next two days. Same thing for hostels and campgrounds. It was also fun to recap the day and send in my update and photos to the newspaper. If the scenery was above average or if the town was interesting, I spent some extra time walking or sitting outside. The TV became less and less important, other than for weather reports. Most nights I slept well, and usually woke energized and excited about the next ride.

Physically, I felt surprisingly strong throughout. A minor hip pointer after a night camping lingered for a few days. I had repetitive soreness in my upper arms and shoulders. I think this came from gripping the handlebars so forcefully as I pedaled hard up the hills. By gripping the handlebars, I seemed to be able to push harder on the pedals with my quads. After the end of a hard climbing day, my arms would be extremely tired.

Following the ride, I was diagnosed with a severe ear infection that had probably been around for the last 3-4 weeks of the trip. One week after returning home, I passed a significant kidney stone. Kidney stones have been a part of my life for many years, but the color and shape of this one was different than usual. My urologist said that he expected that dehydration over the 54 days of the ride was the cause. Two days after passing that stone, I was diagnosed with another one that I must have passed, too.

One concern going into the ride was whether my surgically repaired knee would hold over the grueling ride. Not only did it hold up, the knee is now much stronger. I have more flexibility, especially on stairs.

I was concerned about how nearly two complete months and 4,164 miles of continuous bike riding would affect my running. My first attempt at running came two days after the last bike day. I was amazed that my body and especially my legs seemed to have forgotten most of the running technique that it had done repetitively for more than 30 years. My first run was terrible and I had problems with form and breathing. My legs wanted to spring upward instead of forward. My arms seemed out of place and not sure how to help any forward motion. Posture was also a challenge because I wanted to lean too far forward. With over 70,000 miles of running in my lifetime, I had no idea that I couldn't just jump back on the horse and go. Now after a month of training, my results are somewhat better but not yet back to normal. The ear infection and upper respiratory congestion still linger even after using two different types of prescribed medication. My resting pulse is 10-15 percent higher than it was before the ride, possibly suggesting a long-term holdover from the grueling ride. When coaching my running clients, especially those of a certain level, I use their resting pulse rates to monitor the level of training recovery needed.

The end result of physical portion of my ride was a loss of aerobic capacity. As a longtime runner, I didn't worry too much about being able to ride the bike for long periods each day. However, along the way, some of that aerobic conditioning left me. Runners can't coast on their rides and aren't known for pulling over for a rest on a particularly challenging stretch. I am gradually rebuilding that aerobic capacity. It remains my opinion that long distance runners are in better shape physically than long-distance cyclists. I do credit my training as a runner for the capacity to endure the ride, mentally and physically. My training will now consist of running and biking together, garnering the best of both worlds.

Once the ride ended, I have been asked to speak to various organizations. During the question and answer segment, the following questions always seem to come up. Would you do it again? What would you do differently? Did you feel threatened? And one of my favorites: what did you learn about humanity along the way?

Here are my answers.

Would I do it again? Absolutely, I will go on another long bike ride. Since the TransAmerica Trail is considered the ultimate cross-country ride, I will count it as done and move on to another ride. My first thoughts are that I would like to ride eventually in another country, but before that I will undertake another significant ride in the United States. I knew before leaving on this adventure that I wanted to see more of America and see it in a way that allows close contact. Cycling does just that for me. Next, I hope to ride the East Coast of the United States, possibly Maine to the Florida Keys.

What would I do differently? I will order the Adventure Cycling maps again, but I won't be as closely tied to them in the future. The Adventure Cycling maps need updating. The course is still similar to the 1976 Bicentennial Trail, and I consider that a good thing. However, on my recent trip, I had a great time exploring the Abraham Lincoln sites. Such a trip gains meaning for me by visiting nearby locations that have some historic or other value. I missed Dodge City, Kansas, and the thoroughbred horse country of Kentucky even though I was close to both. My own confidence eventually allowed me to try some off-route exploration, and I wish that I had done more.

Did I feel threatened? Not once on the whole trip did I feel threatened by anything other than high traffic situations. Others, even law-enforcement officers, warned me to carry a gun. Others frankly said that I was crazy to do this ride, especially alone. People never worried me, and neither did situations that I encountered. It was all part of the grand adventure. I mentioned in an earlier chapter that I carried a heavy cable bike lock but never used it. I also mentioned that it won't be included on my next ride. The real reason why is that I want to do my part to trust others, have faith in them and count on them too as I did on my final ride to the beach in South Carolina. I could have worried excessively about heavy traffic behind me but I eventually left that worry with God and

177

rode on. I marveled at how the traffic found a way to let me have my three-foot safety cushion on the side of the highway. It was yet another example of my favorite theme, "Lord, ride with me today."

What did I learn about humanity along the way? I found that America is still stocked with some of the most caring and wonderful people from coast to coast. Yes, I knew to keep my eyes open and will continue to be aware of situations around me. But my real take away from this ride is that the people make our country great, and they made this adventure worth doing. The scenery, especially in the western states, took my breath away. However, as the ride developed, I yearned more and more to meet and talk to the individuals along the way. There are so many to name that I won't even try for fear of leaving out someone. I am convinced that the greatest asset of the United States is still its people. Genuine and caring people are around every corner and in every magnificent little town. I will always remember those folks who took time to talk with me while I experienced my great adventure.

I've mentioned my Top Ten List of Small Towns. Here it is:
1. Kremmling, Colorado
2. Kooskia, Idaho
3. Hutchinson, Kansas
4. Pittsburg, Kansas
5. Cambridge, Ohio
6. Ellington, Missouri
7. Hazard, Kentucky
8. Whiteville, Kentucky
9. Darby, Montana
10. Ness City, Kansas
Honorable Mentions: Marion, Kentucky; Damascus, Virginia; Saratoga, Wyoming

A lot of people have been curious about the total cost of my trip. Without going too far into specifics, total cost was just over $6,000. This doesn't include the cost of the bike since it will be used hopefully for more rides. Some of the gear will too, but nothing seems as permanent as the bike. Cost of motels, hostels, food and liquids, one airline ticket and the gear that I carried on this trip make up the total expenditure. In my mind, seeing the country at the pace I did was well worth the cost. I would tell anyone that this was the best money I have ever spent on travel.

ONGOING MEDICAL ISSUES
— The ride was obviously harder
than I thought —

Now three months since the end of the ride, I am still deep in various medical issues. In order, there was a broken tooth suffered in Alma, Colorado, then kidney stones, shortness of breath, an ear infection, an acute deep vein thrombosis with additional issues and finally the discovery of a brain tumor.

Preface these medical issues with almost perfect health for many years prior to my cross country ride. My doctor said, "You don't even come in when you need to." Honestly, other than a few kidney stones over the last five years, I had only visits for physicals. That has changed dramatically now. I have found out much more about hospitals, the medical process and dealing with insurance issues.

At the end of the ride, August 4, 2013, I expected to get off the bike and rest for a day or two. I was happy with sitting on the beach for just one day. My first attempt at running again came on the morning of August 6, and I found my muscles to be very un-cooperative. My only goal was to run at least two miles, yet still I hoped for three. My running form was terrible, with my posture and foot strikes very inefficient. My legs just simply didn't want to go forward, but seemed to prefer pushing me up in the air. This was probably a result of all the quadriceps strengthening from climbing endless hills. With all this going on, I expected just a minor decrease in stamina. What I found was a struggle to breathe normally. In the beginning, I just thought that the challenge of the long ride had worn my body down.

After arrival back home, I almost immediately passed a fairly large kidney stone, and just two days later felt another one. I visited my urologist and he pegged the cause as dehydration. That seemed to fit because there were certainly many long and hot days on the bike in July. I must have passed the second one quickly too, though I didn't know for sure when I did.

Next came some work on the broken tooth, and a resulting plan to have a crown installed, my first in many years. I decided to not hold the broken tooth against Alma, Colorado, but still wondered what would have happened if anything other than bar food had been available.

Then things got serious. My breathing continued to worsen. I found that even minor exertion was causing me problems. I had resumed working with my running clients, but then struggled as my breathing became more labored. Several became alarmed when I couldn't complete our workouts. I was worried too, and began regular visits to my physician's assistant. He chose to repeat the physical that I had taken just a week before the beginning of my ride.

The process to determine the cause of my breathing problems included an x-ray, EKG, echocardiogram and more blood work. The medical folks suggested that I was just simply worn out from the ride. I took a few days off from running and quickly found out that this didn't help. I was worried, especially once a heart problem called cardiomyopathy was mentioned.

The next Sunday evening, after a deep pain in my right calf worsened for three days, I suddenly wondered if a blood clot might be the problem. After searching for information on symptoms, I became convinced that I had a blood clot because most of the symptoms were present. Rapid and often racing pulse, shortness of breath, unexplained pain in the lower leg and calf, dizziness and coughing for no apparent reason all fit perfectly. I made notes and was waiting when my doctor's office opened on Monday morning. The staff got me in to see my P.A., and I had to convince him that I could have a clot. He said, "Healthy people don't have blood clots." My research showed that it was a common issue for endurance cyclists, particularly those who spent significant time at elevation. The P.A. agreed to send me for an ultrasound after much discussion.

Just 20 seconds into the test, an acute deep vein thrombosis (blood clot) was discovered in my right leg.

After finding the clot in my leg, the doctors suggested a lung scan to see if there were also clots there. The CT scan did find more clots in my lungs, commonly called pulmonary embolisms. I returned to the doctor's office where suggestions were made on how to proceed. More than one medical person reminded me that I was lucky to be alive.

I got a shot and a prescription for blood thinners on the same day, and was also scheduled for an abdominal CT and a brain MRI. Both procedures would look for more clots. I was also scheduled to visit with an oncologist/hematologist for more extensive blood work. Most of this seemed like overkill to me. I later found out it was not.

Within a week, because of the resulting MRI, a tumor was found in the ventricle section of my brain. More blood work was ordered and I was scheduled to visit a neurosurgeon.

The additional blood work has come back completely normal, much different than the tumor. The tumor is rare, and the neurosurgeon has suggested that we watch it for six months before any action is taken. The chief neuroradiologist at the hospital even suggested that it might be a "flow artifact," which is not a tumor at all but simply looks like one.

A second opinion from a neurologist with an imagery specialty has been scheduled. The blood clots, now thought of as being caused by prolonged dehydration and extensive time at elevation, are being treated. My breathing has improved greatly, and the last several weeks included an average of fifty running miles and normal farm work. I am not supposed to be running a chain saw because of the blood thinner, but I am being extra careful when I do.

It may be several weeks or months, or possibly years, before all of these issues are cleared up. Though the bike ride played a huge part in many of the health problems discussed in this chapter, the bike ride also led to the early detection of the brain tumor. I still consider my cross country bike ride to be the adventure of a lifetime and wouldn't have missed it for anything short of a family emergency. My plans for another long distance ride are already taking shape.

EPILOGUE
— A humbling return —

My bike ride across the country took 54 days of pedaling. The experience of the ride is something that I will never forget. I spend time reflecting on the trip each day, and I realize that the biggest reward is much larger than anything that I have accomplished.

Climbing the 11,500-foot Hoosier Pass in Colorado was extremely rewarding. So was riding along in the Wind River Canyon in Wyoming, with endless spectacular rock walls that change colors from sun and clouds before your eyes. I can't forget climbing the mountains that overlook the Pacific Ocean, and hoping to sight a whale.

I met Mountain Man, who hopes to be lowered into the Ohio River while chained in a locked casket. I also met an Illinois man who makes a believable claim to be a close blood relative of Elvis. There were the two young men, one Chinese and one German, who both made their first trips to America to ride across this great country on a bike.

Little towns captured my heart: Kremmling, Colorado; Dubois, Wyoming; Darby, Montana; and so many more. Of course, what made these towns so special was the people who live in them.

People went out of their way to do things for me. Joe, the bike repair guy, fixed my bike at his house late one evening and wanted to charge me less than the cost of parts. There was the convenience store owner who let me camp behind her store and made me a meal just before she closed for the night. I can't forget the surveyor who had water when I needed it more than I probably ever had. There were many more.

Back on June 10, 2013, my ride started way out in the farthest point of Oregon near Astoria. I flew across the country on what should have been an easy day. Because of plane issues, just getting there was a frustrating event and my start was delayed by a half day. On the first climb out of Astoria, I struggled so much that just getting to the top was all I could do. This was a small hill compared to those that I would climb later. Few people knew that I had two accidents the first week, both resulting in some scrapes and bloody fingers but nothing more serious. Everything worked out, though, and the trip exceeded all of my expectations.

All of these, and so many more rewards made up the most exciting adventure of my life. But the greatest reward from my journey is none of the above. Just before I left, a few folks told me that they would be following along. I received regular messages in the early weeks of the ride from friends who offered hope and prayers that all would go well. Those messages increased as the weeks continued, but they were still from people who I expected might follow along as I proceeded east.

Just a few weeks into the journey, I had an idea that others might be keeping up. Salisbury Post Editor Elizabeth Cook planned an ice cream reception, although I wondered if anyone would come. On the rainy afternoon that I arrived home, most people didn't know it because they were following the newspaper reports that ran a day behind. Actually, I didn't know what day I would arrive home until early that same afternoon, so it was a surprise, even to me. Messages came in wishing me the best to make it home. It seemed that possibly some folks were keeping up.

Nothing was complete until the two-day ride to the beach, and I cautioned everyone that the ride in that beach traffic could be a big challenge. With more prayers and a little luck, the final ride went even better than expected. It was rewarding to see the ocean come in sight on Third Avenue in Myrtle Beach, and to dip the worn front tire into the waves.

The most important reward still remained, and it began to fall into place when I was back home and at the Post reception. I was humbled and remain so as I continue to hear from so many of the residents of Rowan County and surrounding areas, and now other states that followed along, keeping up with my progress. All of your thoughts, hopes and prayers helped to get me back home. Very simply, thank you for my biggest reward! I am so glad that you were riding along. I appreciate it more than I can ever express.

A LESSON IN PERSEVERANCE

When local columnist David Freeze announced his intention to ride a bicycle all the way across the country this summer, it sounded like a formidable challenge. And when he offered to send daily updates with photos to publish in the Salisbury Post, editors were happy to accept them.

But it wasn't until he dipped the back wheel of his bike in the Pacific and set off, sharing his experiences day by day, that the real magnitude of what Freeze was attempting became clear to those back home. It was a long solo journey through all kinds of terrain and weather.

Post readers were right there with Freeze as he covered more than 4,100 miles, climbing steep mountains and crossing windy plains, going through cold rain at one point and, just days later, heat so fierce that sweat dripped off his elbows.

Those who followed his travels sent up prayers and emailed encouraging messages. Many of us worried about him. We could envision him, sharing narrow roads with wide trucks and going long, lonely stretches without any place to buy food or water for miles and miles.

Speaking of food, while we read of his adventures from the comfort of our desks and easy chairs, Freeze was burning 7,000 calories a day, hauling up to 40 pounds of supplies and pedaling 10 hours a day.

We learned a lot about the country, and we learned a lot about Freeze — including what he likes to eat. Pancakes, Pop-Tarts and pizza. Brownies and bananas. And ice cream, ice cream, ice cream. Though Freeze was not much of an ice cream eater before the trip, the frozen dessert hit the spot like nothing else on this trip. He even started using the phrase, "my first ice cream of the day."

Hence the decision to serve ice cream at a reception for Freeze on Wednesday. The Post invited readers to come congratulate him on successfully completing the journey, and they embraced him like family. He had dipped his front wheel in the Atlantic on Sunday, showing us all what it means to tackle an audacious goal, persevere through all conditions, keep a positive outlook and reach the goal. Thank you, David Freeze, for taking us all along for the journey.

Salisbury Post
August 13, 2013

Reprinted with permission

CPSIA information can be obtained at www.ICGtesting.com
Printed in the USA
BVOW04s2138241113

337058BV00003B/3/P